SERVANT LEADERSHIP

DISCOVER THE 10 ESSENTIAL SKILLS TO UNLOCK YOUR TEAM PERFORMANCE AND BECOME AN AMAZING SERVANT LEADER

ROBERT STEWART

TABLE OF CONTENTS

ABOUT THE AUTHOR

I'm a Team Leader with more than 20 years of expertise, and my name is Robert Stewart. Leadership and how to enhance the performance of my teams have always piqued my attention. I've had positions as a line manager, a top manager, and I presently run one of the most significant businesses in the world.

I want to thank you for buying this book. Although you could have chosen any number of books to read, you chose this one, and I am very appreciative of that.

I hope it made your daily life a little bit better and more valuable.

I'd love to hear from you if you appreciate this book and get anything from reading it, and I really hope you'll take the time to leave an Amazon review. Your suggestions and encouragement will enable the author to significantly hone his writing skills for next projects and enhance the quality of this book.

I want you, the reader, to know how essential your review is, so if you'd like to submit one, all you have to do is scan the QR code and you're done.

 I'm hoping for the best for your future achievements!

INTRODUCTION

Despite few exceptions, wolves are often pack animals. They are a pack of different wolves that band together to achieve one common objective: survival. Leaders, hunters, carers, and sentinels are just a few of the roles played by different animals in the society. Each member of the pack has a certain function, and each wolf is responsible for that function. The wolves that do not behave in accordance with their role are often excluded from the pack and labeled "lone wolves."

A wolf pack must shift from one hunting territory to another when food sources grow scarce in order to secure the survival of each individual pack member. Contrary to popular belief, the wolves' largest and strongest leaders are not at the front leading the pack when the group starts to move. Instead, wolves get together to establish a protective community. The wolves may have the capacity to plan ahead thanks to years of evolution that have given them a sense of foresight. The smaller, younger, and older wolves are often positioned at the head of the pack while the bigger, stronger wolves take up places all about the pack to guarantee its safety and survival. With this method, the wolves may travel more easily while also safeguarding the group from outside threats. Wolves seem to have a feeling of belonging that enables them to show empathy by defending the smaller, weaker wolves when the pack is on the move.

It might be challenging to keep the pack together as they go between hunting spots since there are hazards around every bend. The strongest wolves stay at the back of the pack, leading the other wolves in the proper path and communicating with them via growls, barks, and howls. The wolves known as sentinels, who wander along the pack's border while instinctively keeping their eyes and ears open, are basically listening and scanning the trees for danger. In the centre of the pack, snuggled together, nursing wolves, young pups, and old wolves assist one another on their trip.

Although we are not wolves, humans are social beings in many respects. In general, we need to feel that we are a part of an organization or a cause that is more important than any one person. We are born into a little familial unit. We attend school, form friendship groups, and ultimately join the workforce where we discover ourselves a part of several groups, whether they are task colleagues or lunch buddies. In every organization, a natural leader emerges to direct the group's activities. Even if there may be some disagreement, the leader ultimately chooses what everyone will do—what the group's objective will be. In various situations, the leader is either a dictatorial figure who says, "Let's all do this" or "I don't want us to do that," or a servant leader who considers the opinions of the group as a whole before making decisions. In the end, a servant leader often achieves better and more fruitful outcomes than a dictatorial leader because the group is happy, everyone is working toward a shared goal, and everyone feels valued and supported in their responsibilities.

CHAPTER 1

ON LEADERSHIP

"It is better to lead from behind and to put others in front, especially when you celebrate victory when nice things occur. You take the front line when there is danger. Then people will appreciate your leadership." – Nelson Mandela

Despite not being wolves, we are sociable creatures. People want connection and a sense of inclusion in a greater whole. Anytime two or more individuals get together and form groups, they inevitably stratify into distinct positions. There are always the idea people, the support people, the debate makers, and the people who like to simply hang around, even in groups of close friends. Friends may not form the foundation of a huge organization, but the same fundamental stratification principles still hold true: corporate board (the "idea" friends), executive staff, support staff, and "ground floor" employees.

There is much more to becoming a leader than simply having charisma and charm. Not everyone who is sociable and surrounds themselves with others qualifies as a leader. All one has to do to create a cult of personality is to be approachable and likeable. Unfortunately, this causes problems since people are unpredictable and prone to change; a leader who cannot keep up with this or who does not remain loyal to who they are and what they believe in will fail.

Transformative and transactional leaders are the two primary categories of leaders in general (Types of Leadership Styles/Maryville Online, 2020). The most fundamental kind of leadership is transactional leadership, which entails a "trade" between the leader and their followers. Typically, a paycheck is used to complete this transaction. According to this notion, team members agree to follow their leader's instructions and complete all work "as given," which has the benefit of outlining everyone's obligations and establishing clear expectations for each team member. People who are typically ambitious and those driven by external rewards—like money, awards, or maybe a diploma for some—often prosper in this model since the transactional leader is based on performance. The drawback is that for many, this causes poor morale among followers and a high rate of group churn. One can only increase employee performance so much with this kind of leadership, which stifles innovation and discourages personal development.

Transformational leadership is a trend that is gaining traction in business and other organizations. A transformational leader's primary trait is a constant search for innovation and advancement (Types of Leadership Styles/Maryville Online, 2020). As a transactional leader would, a transformational leader delegated tasks and responsibilities. Despite the fact that everyone has a part to play, a transformational leader attempts to push their people beyond what is anticipated. A transformational leader encourages others by fostering and promoting the professional and personal development of their followers. Simply said, transformational leaders set an example for others to follow in order to improve themselves and their communities. They construct a moral code for their group, which everyone adheres to. They establish unambiguous, moral norms and work to uphold them all the time. They cultivate a culture that inspires their adherents and others to prioritize the welfare of others above their own interests. A transformational model educates and guides followers on how to make decisions and take ownership of their actions.

Beyond only transactional and transformational leadership, psychologist Kurt Lewin and his colleagues set out to find more leadership philosophies in 1939. (Cherry, 2020). In this research, Lerwin divided schoolchildren into three groups, each of which was headed by a different kind of leader. The youngsters in each group were then guided through an arts and crafts activity, and researchers watched how they behaved. Lewin was able to distinguish three leadership philosophies from this research: authoritarian, democratic, and laissez-faire. Lewin's research served as the foundation for subsequent leadership studies that served as a launchpad for more elaborate leadership theories.

Authoritarian (Autocratic) Leadership

When the government uses this paradigm, it is referred to be a dictatorship. Traditionally top-down leadership is most often linked with this type of leadership in non-governmental organizations. In this model, the leader retains total authority over every area of the business, often prescribing what must be done, when it must be done, and the precise procedures that must be taken to execute a task. This paradigm has advantages, and it works best in short-term circumstances. In this concept, the authoritarian leader is seen as an authority. All judgments may be made swiftly once this is kept in mind. In an emergency, this is very critical. When dealing with emergency or crisis circumstances, many companies that do not use this style of leadership have developed a "chain of command" or authoritarian model outside of the typical group environment.

Making decisions is also more effective using this strategy. Analysis paralysis is not an issue if just one person is in charge of making choices and managing daily operations. Simply speaking, having too many individuals involved in the decision-making process leads to analysis paralysis. The conclusions reached in a collaborative decision-making process will always be subject to dispute. The decision-making process will come to a screeching stop as group members study and debate the potential repercussions of a choice as a result of these persistent objections from others.

As a result, even while this approach may be advantageous for the purpose of efficiency, it has drawbacks. The supporters of autocratic leaders often see them as being oppressive and tyrannical. Group members often experience resentment and distrust toward the leader as a result of the leader's exclusion from the decision-making process, which prevents followers from developing professionally and dictates all elements of the organization's daily operations.

Tight deadlines are the life and death of the news business, especially print journalism. A highly strict deadline must be met for the writing, editing, and typing of news stories. Due to the industry's strict restrictions, an autocratic/authoritative style is practically required. What might happen when an authoritarian leader pushes their supporters too far is shown by the case of Howell Raines. The New York Times' executive editor was Raines (2001-2003). As the executive editor, it was his responsibility to control the budget, assign content to writers, and produce a newspaper that readers would want to purchase. Without consulting his team or the journalists, Raines assigned topics that he believed would be significant at the moment; he was a true dictatorial boss. He had alienated a significant portion of his personnel due to his aggressive, "my way or the highway" attitude. Joe Sexton, the deputy editor, went to the board members to let them know that the employees felt bullied rather than led, as an example of this. Additionally, senior staff employees protested, informing the board that Raines was feared rather than appreciated. He was eventually made to go, but it was too late since a sizable portion of the workforce felt alienated and many of them departed the newspaper for other chances (Fata, 2019).

Democratic (Participatory) Leadership

According to Lewin (1939), democratic leadership is one of the best leadership philosophies since it encourages followers to participate more actively in the decision-making process. Everyone is welcome to engage in this manner. The leader promotes a process in which their followers are urged to take part, engage in idea exchange, and conduct internal analysis of these ideas. Despite the democratic leader's propensity to emphasize equality among group members and the free exchange of ideas, the leader is nevertheless there to provide direction and control (Rose Ngozi Amanchukeo et al., 2015).

While everyone in the group is urged to engage, the leader is entrusted with selecting who joins the group and who gets to make decisions. By enabling everyone in the group to participate in the decision-making process, this leadership does lend itself to increasing productivity and strengthening the morale of the group. However, the choice is ultimately made by the leader. Democratic leaders seek out the opinions and ideas of their followers while respecting and upholding their own ideals and moral convictions. Democratic leaders are also aware of the importance of divergent viewpoints and treat them with the same respect as their own.

Democratic leaders come under fire when their followers (workers) lack knowledge, expertise, or experience, and when communication channels are limited. Group members who lack the knowledge or expertise necessary to participate in decision-making or who are confused about their roles and responsibilities further complicate this problem. Additionally, enabling group members to participate in decision-making increases the feeling of ownership among followers and produces more ideas; yet, it does tend to slow down procedures as everyone participating evaluates and provides feedback on the current situation.

The democratic leadership approach resembles a sports team since everyone is working together for the greater benefit. There are exceptions, but this kind of leadership is often used by executive staff or small groups. Twitter might be considered a team effort. All four founders of the new social networking platform—Jack Dorsey, Biz Stone, Evan Williams, and Noah Glass—had an equal voice in its conception. Because of the network's participatory design, this group effort is open to all of its users. Everyone on the network collaborates or participates in some way, and according to Dorsey, users may influence decisions by simply "tweeting" their views and ideas for how they believe Twitter should develop (Gamelearn Team, 2016).

Laissez-Faire (Delegative) Leadership

According to Lewin's study, groups of kids with delegative leadership were the least effective (Lewin, 1939). Lewin also discovered that these kids were incapable of working independently, put greater expectations on the leader, and exhibited minimal teamwork. Lewin noted that teams led by laissez-faire employees lacked direction and held one another accountable for failures. Additionally, group members performed less work and made less progress while refusing to take accountability for their acts or themselves.

The ability to delegate effectively calls for a great deal of confidence. A group's leader has to have faith that every participant is capable of carrying out their assigned tasks without the need for micromanagement. This kind of leadership is characterized by "hands-off" behavior from the leader, who provides little to no direction to the group. Group members are expected to work independently to find solutions to challenges, even while the delegative leader offers the necessary tools and resources. When group members are highly talented, driven, and capable of working autonomously with little to no supervision, a laissez-faire approach might be helpful. People with intrinsic motivation flourish under this kind of leadership. Instead of being driven by something external like money, people are motivated by an inside feeling of fulfillment (a paycheck). When group participants have greater expertise than the leader, this specific approach works well (Al Malki & Juan, 2018). Members of the group may show off their knowledge and abilities using this format.

When group members lack the knowledge or abilities required for their roles, this leadership style is inappropriate. This leadership style is bad for followers who struggle with deadlines, project management, or who are incapable of handling problems. Delegative leadership in general and delegative leaders in particular are often seen as being ineffective or hardly involved with the group. In this regard, the group's lack of cohesion is caused by the leader's seeming lack of interest in what is occurring. Additionally, some leaders use this approach to escape accountability for the failure of the organization. When objectives aren't achieved, it's simpler to point the finger at the group than it is to accept responsibility for one's own shortcomings.

The laissez-faire leadership approach is often used by governmental organizations. Governments are enormous organizations entrusted with upholding public safety and ensuring the efficient operation of the government. In this instance, the government disregards residents' wishes; if someone wants to plant a tree in their yard, they don't need to seek permission from the authorities.

Affiliate Leadership

One of the most emotive leadership philosophies is affiliate leadership, which is closely related to laissez-faire leadership. Affiliate leaders try to develop and strengthen emotional bonds with their followers by appealing to their emotions. This is accomplished through positive reinforcement with the focus of making everyone—followers and leaders alike—feel supported, valued, and heard (Tobin, 2020). An affiliate leader's main objectives are to demonstrate empathy, tolerance, and a dedication to peaceful dispute resolution. Rather than dealing with group conflicts on a professional level, the affiliate leader attempts to understand the emotional roots of the problem and resolve them on a personal level. Additionally, affiliate leaders take a more flexible approach, allowing their followers to consider alternatives and collaborate with team members to either find solutions or ask their manager to request help or a more flexible schedule. In contrast, some leadership styles rely on rigid schedules, policies, and procedures.

This fashion does offer certain benefits. Many leaders discover that this strategy boosts followers' morale because they feel appreciated and respected (Tobin, 2020). In general, followers are happier and work more at their duties when they feel appreciated and respected. Additionally, it fosters a feeling of confidence in the leader and the organization when leaders take the worries of their followers into account. This, in turn, encourages the followers to want to do more in the leader's, the organization's, and their' best interests. Like delegatory leadership, affiliate leadership employs a hands-off style of management, working to create a setting where followers feel free to take the initiative and operate independently. Affiliate leadership, although beneficial in certain ways, has a number of drawbacks as well, which serve to stimulate creativity and ingenuity in problem-solving. This kind of leadership involves the leader trying to motivate followers by evoking good emotions, lavish praise, and "happy thoughts." Affiliate leaders avoid confrontation and hard situations because they want to keep everyone happy. In turn, this causes the leader to lose sight of the group's aim or goal. Conflict may also arise when a leader's opinion is discounted or disregarded while assessing a follower's performance. Team output will often suffer if an affiliate leader spends too much time attending to the emotional needs of their members. What is the motivation to do better if average performance is "good enough" in this regard?

Pacesetting Leadership

Pacesetting leadership, as first defined by Daniel Goleman in his 2010 book Emotional Intelligence: Why it Can Matter More Than IQ, is one that combines a desire to complete projects and a drive to complete goals (Money-zine.com, 2020). Doing as I do, now is one of the best ways to comprehend pacesetting leadership. Pacesetters have high expectations for both themselves and their followers. In this way, the leader does set an example for others to follow. Typically, a pacesetter leader won't ask others to do anything they won't do first. By their very nature, pacesetting leaders are relentless, demanding, and even exacting (Raiz, 2019).

There are a few benefits to this style of leadership. Setting the pace for their team may help them do their best work, but only temporarily. Given the characteristics of a pacesetter, followers are often like-minded, very skilled, and competent specialists in their fields who can complete a given job with minimal input or guidance supplied.

The drawback of pacesetting leadership is that it often backfires on the team. The expectations placed on followers, along with a constantly shifting environment, may soon overwhelm them. Ironically, pacesetting leaders often leave their followers perplexed and upset because they lack tolerance for individuals who need to learn or aren't picking up a skill fast enough, in addition to not taking the time to provide feedback. When a leader sets the pace, those who can't keep up are promptly removed with little to no opportunity to become better (Money-zine, 2020).

Jack Welch is an example of a trend-setting leader who is both highly contentious and well-respected for his accomplishments. He is noted for leading GE through one of its most prosperous times while serving as CEO from 1981 to 2001. Redesigning the GE labor structure was one of Welch's first moves. In contrast to the worst 10% of performance, he dismissed the bottom 20% of performers and awarded the top 20%. Welch was a serious individual who surrounded himself with the top specialists he could locate. This enabled Welch to maintain a low-key approach while the business expanded (Sharma, 2013).

Coaching Leadership

This design differs slightly from the others. The coaching leader encourages their followers to try something new on their own, in contrast to other leadership models that place more emphasis on instructing, demonstrating how to do something, or directly assigning work (Miller, 2018). Coaching leaders attempt to demonstrate to their followers how they, and their work, fit into the larger scheme of the organization. In essence, the coaching leader shows how their followers are pieces of a puzzle, and how each piece needs to be successfully completed for the puzzle to be completed. This model makes a constant effort to solicit feedback, both positive and negative. In order to foster an environment where followers are encouraged and rewarded for enhancing their personal and professional strengths, coaching leaders use empathy and self-awareness. A coaching leader doesn't withhold information and is open and helpful, especially when assessing a follower's overall performance. As a result, followers always know what is expected of them.

The mentoring-style relationship between the leader and the follower is a key component of the coaching leadership model. There is no ambiguity because expectations for the team and the individual are made clear right away. The organization encourages and mentors followers to develop their personal skills through this mentoring process. A side benefit of this type of mentoring is that as followers are continuously coached and new skills are learned, it promotes the development of future leaders within the organization.

The coaching leadership model, on the other hand, takes a lot of time. Developing followers' trust and providing them with new skills takes time. Many organizations may not always benefit from this level of commitment; the time commitment alone is too great, and many may not be in a position to be able to make such commitments.

Leaders who coach others must possess strong leadership qualities and be aware that mentoring is not always the best strategy.
The talents of a coach leader determine how successful they can
be. The issues that might arise when a coaching leadership style
is used improperly or ineffectively may be insurmountable.
When a leader exerts more effort than the individual being
mentored, the situation may improve in certain cases, but it
produces an imbalanced equation that leads to dissatisfaction
and disappointment. Coaching is a partnership between a leader
and a follower; without the follower's commitment, the coach is
unable to influence them.

CHAPTER 2
WHY SERVANT LEADERSHIP?

"The purpose of human life is to serve, and to show compassion and the will to help others." - Albert Schweitzer

J eff inhaled deeply as he entered his new workplace and started to consider the challenges that lay ahead. Jeff was taking on his first managerial position in his young career after just receiving his MBS and being employed as a corporate recruit. He had been appointed to manage a group that was renowned as a "problem." His boss had forewarned Jeff about the gang. There were "too many managers and not enough employees," he informed Jeff. To put it another way, nobody on the team had taken the time to pause and consider the requirements of the other individuals. This often occurs in the world of business. People let their egos, as well as their desire for fame and success, rule over what ought to be common sense. Although it may seem cliche, the term "team" does not include a "I." Throughout his master's degree, Jeff had studied several management and leadership philosophies, and he was prepared to put his knowledge to use.

Anyone who has ever been a member of a team, whether it was in sports, business, or anything else, has encountered a variety of leadership styles, some of which were effective and others which weren't. We get knowledge from those who guide us as we mature and integrate into our societies (micro and macro). We discover the qualities of leaders we value and those we do not. More importantly, we discover how humans react to different leadership philosophies and which philosophies are most effective.

Although they are partly connected, authority and power are fundamentally separate concepts in a leadership dynamic. One takes a leader to win over and win over the group, while the other comes about as a consequence of displaying power by intimidation or terror. While assuming control and forcing a team to conform to one's way may be the quickest solution, the outcome is often a poisonous atmosphere that promotes resentment and dread rather than teamwork and community.

In this regard, the power leadership style is by its very nature a dictatorial one. A power-style leader just ignores the process and focuses on the outcome. A power-style leader will disregard other people's opinions and assert their own expertise, forcing team members to modify the majority, if not all, of their work to suit the leader's objectives.

Sarah eagerly anticipated taking charge of "her" business as a young, just appointed shift manager for a modest female boutique in the mall. When Sarah took over as manager, she convened a staff meeting to introduce herself and let everyone know that there was "a new sheriff in town" and that things would be changing. Sarah continued by describing herself as a "no-nonsense" boss who ultimately held the reins of authority and whose word was definitive. She told her prospective employees at the conclusion of the meeting that they were "free to quit at any moment" if they disagreed with anything she said or the way she operated the shop.

Being appointed for a leadership role does not automatically give one the power to lead. This is complex and challenging; it calls for a whole different way of thinking about leadership than what is often accepted. It takes work to gain the right to lead. In this sense, a leader has to gain the esteem of their subordinates or community. Now the issue is, "How does a leader get the power to lead?" This is where the idea of the servant leader comes from.

The idea of servant leadership is not quite new. This kind of thinking has been used by many great thinkers and leaders throughout history to further the goals of a society or organization. Chinese philosopher Laozi, who lived in the fifth century B.C., described the idea of servant leadership. Laozi thought that the ideal leader was one who focused on the people instead of himself. The people shout, "We accomplished it," as opposed to the leader stating, "I achieved it." Undoubtedly, the teachings of Jesus Christ include some of the most well-known instances of servant leadership.

Although it is not a new concept, servant leadership is a revolutionary action that flips conventional leadership paradigms on its head. A top-down style to leadership is used in many older models; in these models, the team leader is always at the top. On the other side, using a servant leadership approach is known as "leading from behind." In this paradigm, the group leader must have a service-first mentality rather than the team serving the leader. A servant leader strives to uplift and encourage people who report to them so they may realize their full potential. The purpose of the servant leader is for every member of the team or community to feel empowered to assist others, not for self-glorification.

It might be challenging to define servant leadership from an organizational perspective. The idea itself is contradictory; how can one lead while also serving? This is often misinterpreted and runs counter to many contemporary views of leadership. Many leadership theories call for a leader to be strong and "take control," guiding their team in one direction or another. Because they are not leading the team from the front, servant leaders look ineffective and disinterested. Both servant leadership and disengagement are not signs of weakness. Unlike many conventional styles of leadership and management, which place the mission first before concentrating on team member empowerment, servant leaders put the success of their team members first. In this paradigm, the leader and their team serve the mission or community while the servant leaders serve those who report to them. In other words, servant leaders achieve corporate or societal objectives by assisting their subordinates in strengthening their capacities and performing well in their assigned responsibilities.

In transitioning to this approach, leadership circles today use Robert Greenleaf's essay collection "The Servant as Leader" (Greenleaf, 1971). Greenleaf explores a shift in how leadership communicates with people within an organizational group in his article. A leader who adopts this style addresses an issue, business, or community from the perspective of a "servant first" attitude. Instead of seeking personal glory, the servant leader seeks to fulfill the desires and needs of their group, organization, or community. Because it requires humility and putting others' needs before one's own, this kind of leadership is more challenging. However, servant leaders eventually find that group performance "goes through the sky" (Tarallo, 2018).

Greenleaf argued that being a servant leader is a choice throughout all of his works. One must choose to put the needs of others above their own. Leaders have a history of claiming credit for the efforts of their teams. After all, the mission would not have been completed if it weren't for the direction leader. Few people pay recognition to those who support them along the road since everyone wants to be recognized for their successes. General George Patton of the United States is well-remembered, yet no one can identify his secretary. In other words, the demands of the group, group of people, or organization should take precedence over the leader's wants. A leader must have patience and humility in order to do this. The leader is not ultimately the focus of attention. The demands of the team should come first in a servant leader's approach; the whims of the leader are unimportant.

Greenleaf came to the conclusion that conventional power models, which ask, "What can you do for me?" weren't very helpful and produced subpar outcomes. According to Greenleaf, the most effective leaders first address the needs of their communities before addressing the requirements or objectives of an organization. Greenleaf found that the most effective of these leaders had ten fundamental traits:

- Listening

- Empathy

- Healing

- Self-Awareness

- Persuasion

- Conceptualization

- Foresight

- Stewardship

- Commitment to growth

- Building community

CHAPTER 3
LISTENING

"I remind myself every morning: Nothing I say this day will teach me anything. So if I'm going to learn, I must do it by listening." - Larry King

n the past, leaders have shown exceptional communication and decision-making abilities. The ancient Greek philosopher Epictetus reportedly said that because humans have two mouths and ears, we listen twice as much as we talk. Unfortunately, this lesson has been forgotten by a lot of individuals; this is particularly true among managers and supervisors in businesses.

Information travels downward under an authoritarian paradigm. Organizational owners provide management with a mission and educate and lead them as they divide the mission into sections. These pieces are given to supervisors, who divide them into smaller parts and distribute them to other team members. The same thing takes place in neighborhood associations as well. In this paradigm, only the organization's founder or a prominent member of the community may influence the ultimate objective. Additionally, individuals who are in charge of carrying out the job find themselves cut off from it and just "putting in seat time"—working on a project, objective, or aim that has, in the context of a community organization, at best been poorly conveyed and may not assist the people it is supposed to help.

Similar to this, under a laissez-faire strategy, the leader delegated work without explicitly outlining the purpose or methodology of the activity. As a result of followers not knowing what is expected of them and the leader not providing much in the way of explanation, this hands-off style of leadership encourages uncertainty and dissatisfaction. In other words, it is impossible to establish and strengthen the channels of communication. A leader is no longer listening to their followers when they are cut off from them. The leader is not listening to identify problems or to understand the impact of their actions on the company.

Listening is one of the fundamental principles of servant leadership. Great servant leaders see the value of recognizing the opinions of others and listening to every member of their teams or communities. Everyone wants to be heard, but this desire is not mutual. The people doing the tasks at the bottom of the organization often feel ignored and undervalued.

Passive Listening

Communication and decision-making abilities have generally been strong suits for leaders. Man has two ears and a mouth, according to Epictetus, an ancient Greek philosopher, thus we listen twice as much as we talk. Unfortunately, this lesson has been forgotten by a lot of individuals; managers and supervisors in businesses are particularly guilty of this.

Information travels from top to bottom under an authoritarian regime. Organizational owners provide management a mission and educate and lead them on that purpose. The supervisors take those pieces, divide them into smaller portions, and then distribute those parts to other team members. Community groups have the same issue. In this paradigm, the end objective is determined solely by the organization's owner or a prominent member of the community. Additionally, those who are in charge of carrying out the actual work end up being disengaged from it and merely "putting in seat time"—working on a project, mission, or goal that, in the context of a community group, may not benefit the people it is meant to help—and has, at best, been poorly communicated.

Similar to this, in a laissez-faire style, the leader assigns tasks without necessarily explaining the purpose or logistics of the work. Because the leader does not provide many explanations and followers are unclear about what is expected of them, this hands-off style of leadership often results in confusion and discontent. In other words, it is impossible to establish and develop communication channels. A leader that is cut off from their followers is not paying attention to them. The leader is not listening to learn about problems or how their actions are impacting the company.

Listening is one of the cornerstones of servant leadership. Excellent servant leaders see the value of respecting the opinions of other people and listening to all members of their communities or teams. Although it is not reciprocal, everyone wants to be heard. Those at the bottom of the organization—those who are really performing the work—often feel unheard and undervalued.

Active Listening

The servant leader makes a deliberate choice to actively listen in order to better help their communities. Active listening requires the listener to pay close attention, comprehend, react, and recall what is being said. The listener does not only sit and be quiet while engaging in active listening. The person listening actively contributes to the discourse. They are reacting to the speaker's words as well as their actions and nonverbal cues. To have a more thorough knowledge of what is being said, active listening demands a leader to take into account both what is being said and how it is being delivered. The following situations call for active listening: job interviews, roundtable discussions, arguments, counseling, and training.

Active listening uses both verbal and nonverbal listening strategies to show a listener is paying attention to the speaker and actively striving to grasp what is being said, as opposed to passive listening, which requires little to no effort on the listener/part. leader's The two main components of active listening are verbal and nonverbal behaviors.

Eye contact is necessary for nonverbal listening methods, and attention should be given to the other person. In addition to being seated while the topic is being discussed and not fidgeting by doodling, picking their fingernails, or checking their watches or phones, active listeners often nod or lean in. A leader that exhibits these habits is obviously not paying attention, and very simply, it is nasty.

Active listeners are aware that communication requires both parties to participate. A servant leader will give the other person the opportunity to complete their opinion or comment without interjecting. An engaged listener will allow the other person time to reply to a question or remark while keeping in mind that communication is a two-way street and refrain from asking more questions or providing their own answers.

The members of a team or community must develop a feeling of trust in and rapport with the servant leader. An attentive listener will summarize what the other person stated in light of this. This does two things. The first is to show that the speaker was heard, but it also gives the audience a chance to ask questions and provide constructive criticism. It also shows that the speaker's wants and sentiments are taken into consideration by the leader. Active listening also shows a positive outlook and a readiness to adjust to the requirements of the group or community. As a consequence, communication and the desire to actively listen to others help to clarify a subject or issue and validate the thoughts and emotions of individuals who are following the servant leader.

The Apple Computer Company was established on April 1st, 1976, in Cupertino, California, by Steve Job, Ronald Wayne, and

Steve Wozniak (later incorporated as Apple Computers Inc. in 1977). The Apple I, the first item made by the business, was just a motherboard with a processor, memory, and simple text-video chips. The Wozniak-designed Apple I never achieved great success. Apple created a number of high- and low-end computer lines before the end of the 1970s, engaged a complete team of designers and programmers, and started working on the future of computing. Jobs was sure that the point-and-click interface we use today, the Apple Lisa, will be replaced by a visual user interface in the future of computing. Sadly, Lisa turned out to be too expensive, and Jobs was compelled to leave the group and go back to Macintosh. The Macintosh, the first personal computer made without a programming language, was presented by Apple in 1984. Due to the Macintosh's expensive price, poor speeds, and limited software options, sales initially started out well but soon started to decline.

Apple CEO John Sculley fired Steve Jobs as general manager of the Macintosh business as a result of declining sales and internal conflicts. Jobs eventually resigned from the firm in 1985 after Sculley persuaded the Apple Executive team to relieve him of all operational responsibilities.

Apple Computers Inc. was in trouble by the 1990s. Apple has expanded its product range under Sculley to include printers and drawing tablets. They had essentially produced the same system at different price points targeted at various markets, cannibalizing the popular Apple II to start creating more expensive devices. In 1996, Apple rehired Steve Jobs.

Jobs had returned to lead Apple in an effort to reorganize the firm and make it profitable once again. Jobs announced a cooperation with Microsoft as one of his first official actions, humbly telling the 1997 Macworld Expo that "we have to let go of a few things around here if we want to go ahead and see Apple healthy and prosperous again. Let rid of the idea that in order for Microsoft to fail, Apple must win (Shontell, 2011).

Jobs also understood that he need more assistance than merely a collaboration with Microsoft. Jobs invited Tim Cook, a seasoned technologist, to join him at Apple in 1998. Cook had had a successful and lengthy career in the IT industry, spending 12 years at IBM and holding senior roles at Intelligent Electronics and Compaq. Cook declined many overtures from Apple while working at Compaq, but something about Job's tenacity convinced him to accept the meeting. Cook subsequently said that Jobs "built the entire business that I'm in" and that Jobs was "doing something completely different" (Leander Kahney, 2019). Cook joined Apple at a time when few people wanted to work there, morale was poor, and the business was on the verge of going out of business. Cook was chosen by Jobs to be the Senior Vice President of Global Operations. They established a line of contact between the two that permitted an open exchange of thoughts and concerns. Cook "had the same vision I had," according to what Jobs said to the author of the book Steve Jobs. Unless he came and pinged me, we could connect at a high strategic level and I could simply forget about a lot of stuff (Isaacson, 2011).

Steve Jobs paid close attention. Jobs took the executive board's worries about revenue and merchandise into consideration. Stockholders' worries that the value of their shares was falling were heard by Jobs. Jobs paid attention to the worries of the Apple staff. More significantly, he paid attention to Bill Gates, the CEO of Microsoft. He used the lessons from Microsoft's mistakes to improve Apple Computers. He listened to Tim Cook, a well-known computer industry veteran whom Jobs had explicitly chosen to aid in the turnaround of Apple Computer Inc. The iMac, PowerMac, iBook, and Powerbook were the only four basic items he offered. Jobs extended Apple's product range by adding the iPod and later the iPhone as each device gained in quality.

CHAPTER 4

EMPATHY

"Empathy is about finding echoes of another person in yourself." - Mohsin Hamid

Empathy is one of the hardest qualities for a servant leader to master. According to Empathy Definition/What is Empathy (2009), empathy is an emotional quality that enables one to perceive the feelings of others "combined with the capacity to envision what someone else may be thinking or experiencing." Since we are infants, humans have been able to feel the emotions of our caretakers and subsequently express those same feelings in our own way. When our moms are unhappy, we too become unhappy, and vice versa. Understanding that other people's perspectives on the world are quite different from our own requires empathy.

According to researchers, there are three distinct types of empathy that enable individuals to see the world from another person's viewpoint. The first of them is perspective-taking or cognitive empathy. Cognitive empathy is fundamentally the capacity to imagine oneself in another person's situation. This kind of empathy enables a leader to comprehend another's viewpoint without having to interact with their emotions, making it especially helpful for managers or servant leaders in negotiations. This has the drawback of limiting compassion due to cognitive empathy.

Perhaps the most fundamental kind of empathy is emotional empathy. The ability to really experience the feelings of another person is known as emotional empathy. A benefit of emotional empathy is that it enables one to "experience" the feelings of others. Think about those who work in "caring" fields like medicine, education, or social work. The ability to feel other people's emotions helps a doctor react to patients in a helpful way. It also implies that people—more especially, leaders—can react correctly when friends, coworkers, and members of the community show signs of sadness or suffering. When dealing with those that are of a different racial, ethnic, and socioeconomic background than the leader, this kind of empathy may be seen negatively as being too sympathetic and even condescending.

Last but not least, compassionate empathy is the capacity to experience another's suffering, comprehend their feelings, and act to alleviate it. The most suitable kind of empathy is often compassionate empathy, which is what empathy is typically considered to be. Most individuals do not only want to be understood (cognitive empathy) or to have someone else mourn with them (emotional empathy). The majority of people want understanding, empathy for their circumstances, and most crucially, a leader who will act on their behalf or work with them to do so in order to address their problems. Finding a balance is challenging for a servant leader since emotional empathy might be regarded as being too emotional, while cognitive empathy can be seen as being under emotionally.

Daniel Goldman covers a number of important aspects of empathy in his 2010 book, Emotional Intelligence: Why It Can Matter More Than IQ. However, the servant leader strives to empathize with others in order to acquire a deeper feeling of compassion that will enable them to comprehend and effectively respond to others' needs and concerns. It should be mentioned that most individuals do display empathy on some level.

The first person to pinpoint understanding others as a crucial component of empathy was Goldman. The servant leader makes an effort to pick up on others' emotional signals. Active listening and paying attention to nonverbal communication signals make this simple to achieve. Leaders should also be sensitive and try to comprehend other people's viewpoints. To put it another way, a leader shouldn't judge someone until they have personally experienced their perspective, or placed themselves "in another's shoes." Finally, through having a deeper knowledge of others, a servant leader is better able to serve others by focusing on their needs and emotions rather than what the leader "thinks" is best without really comprehending the other person.

According to Goldman, the servant leader should likewise have a service attitude (2010). The classic authoritarian or laissez-faire leadership approach is directly opposed by this notion. In these models, the group leader's direction is the main priority, and teams are formed based on what the members can accomplish to support the leader. This idea is turned on its head by servant leaders. While mostly referring to professional settings, having a service attitude entails prioritizing the needs of the team or community before your own. This is referred to as "going the additional mile" for consumers in the service sector. The servant leader shifts from being merely the boss to more of a trusted counselor when used in a team or community environment.

The servant leader puts others before themselves by working to develop them while keeping this service orientation in mind. According to Goldman, developing others is paying attention to others' needs and concerns before acting on them to help them realize their full potential as both individuals and members of a group or team. In order to foster empathy, a leader should recognize and compliment others for their successes or strengths while offering constructive criticism that will assist others narrow in on how to grow. A leader should also assist their followers attain their greatest potential by mentoring and coaching them. This doesn't always entail giving someone instructions on how to execute a job; rather, it means assisting someone in developing the abilities necessary to complete a task.

Lastly, Goldman cited valuing variety and awareness as essential characteristics of empathy (2010). Simply recognizing that individuals are diverse in terms of their educational backgrounds, worldviews, and personal experiences is celebrating diversity. The servant leader is aware of and appreciates this notion that, despite their differences, all individuals have something valuable to contribute. While embracing diversity, a leader must also be conscious of the emotional ties that run deep within a team or group. Working with persons from different cultural or socioeconomic origins calls for this in particular.

Cultivating Empathy

Empathy development is a challenging process. To experience another's feelings as if they were their own, one must dig deeply inside oneself. While empathy is often innate in most individuals, it may be strengthened and developed through effort. Servant leaders are aware of the challenge and are constantly honing their abilities.

Reading is perhaps one of the simplest methods to develop empathy. Both professors and pupils are present in servant leaders. Reading does, according to research, foster empathy (Schmidt, 2020). Reading is a focused, inward activity. The majority of people read with their eyes, whereas blind individuals use braille and form an image of the tale in their brains. They essentially watch a movie. The reader has to imagine the people in the narrative feeling joy, rage, and sadness since this "movie" represents the brain. People start to comprehend the characters, their goals, and their emotions as they read and "become" the characters. They start to feel sympathy for the characters (Mar, et al., 2005).

Simply challenging oneself is one approach to build empathy. Servant leaders push themselves and engage in frightful situations. They are forced out of their comfort zones by this. It's okay to struggle with a notion or a task. The servant leader puts themselves in the same situation as a struggling follower by striving.

Before speaking, a servant leader must learn to listen, taking in the experiences, worries, and problems of others. Sharing insights on similar experiences after a leader has listened greatly contributes to developing empathy. Both the leader and the follower gain insight and develop a sense of empathy for one another via the sharing of experiences.

One should be conscious of their own prejudices, whether positive or negative. Whether they are aware of it or not, everyone has prejudices; some are subtle and others are overt. A prejudiced and often inaccurate perception of another person based on upbringing or acquired experiences is known as bias. For instance, if a person's earliest memory of a dental visit as a youngster was unpleasant—possibly a traumatic one—that memory will lead that person to have unfavorable biases about dentists. The opposite way around, bias may also be advantageous. One would likely only mention good qualities if asked to describe their partner. This does not imply that one has a flawless spouse, but rather that one's perspective is biased toward the good.

An further skill that a servant leader must develop is empathy; empathy at both the corporate and community levels starts at the top. One must always lead by example as a servant leader; they must put their words into action. Asking open-ended, in-depth questions is one method of developing empathy. For instance, asking a follower, "Tell me more about that," or "I don't understand, can you assist me?" might help a servant leader comprehend their perspective. When things go wrong, this specific approach is really useful. Spend some time thinking about the other person's intentions.

It's important to keep in mind that everyone empathizes differently, whether you're a leader or a follower. Empathy is a talent that must be learned and is unique to each person. Depending on their beliefs, education, social level, and prior experiences, people interpret events in various ways. Due to their disparities, a person from an affluent, educated household and a person from a very impoverished neighborhood would experience the same event in quite different ways. In this situation, politely seeking clarification or further information might aid in understanding one another's viewpoints.

Reed Kennedy has had several Airbnb rejections in 2014. Kennedy, a digital entrepreneur and investor, started to think that his race was the reason he was being turned down. He had a photo of himself on his Airbnb site, and it was probable that his race was a factor in whether or not landlords decided to rent their house to them (Luca & Bazerman, 2020).

Because of how wonderful the Air B&B [sic] we're staying at is, the neighbors mistook us for robbers and contacted the police. (Grant, 2015). In October 2015, the statement and a selfie of a young Black guy named Stefan Grant, which had approximately 3000 retweets, went viral (Griswold, 2020). While playing at a hip-hop concert in Atlanta, Grant and a handful of his buddies rented a house for four people in a quiet suburban area. However, one's capacity for empathy may be increased. A leader may develop their empathy by extremely deliberate and methodical actions and create a culture that supports it.

When discriminatory booking concerns were initially brought up in the case of Airbnb, management's first response was to deny them. They argued that Reed Kennedy's repeated rejections had nothing to do with his color or ethnicity after hearing objections from the corporate representative. The official said that Airbnb hosts have the freedom to refuse booking requests for a reason, and that if the firm had believed that there was a discrimination problem, they would have contacted the hosts (Luca & Bazerman, 2020).

Only after Stefan Grant's tweet gained widespread attention, complaints about unfair booking procedures reached Congress, and a racial discrimination lawsuit was filed in a U.S. district court (Gregory Selden et al. v Airbnb Inc., 2016) did Airbnb decide to take the necessary steps to be more approachable and sympathetic to their clients.

The first step that Airbnb and any servant leader take to develop empathy is to actively listen to their consumers. A month after Grant's post went viral, Airbnb invited him and a buddy to their San Francisco offices to talk about his allegations of discrimination (Griswold, 2016). Airbnb then examined the findings of a Harvard study, which showed that "visitors with distinctly African-American names are 16 percent less likely to have their applications approved compared to equivalent guests with notably White names." Landlords of all sizes experience discrimination, including smaller landlords who share a property and bigger landlords who manage many homes. The discrimination is most obvious among hosts who have never had an African-American visitor, indicating that only a small percentage of hosts engage in it. Although discrimination in rental markets has significantly decreased in recent decades, our findings indicate that Airbnb's present design decisions encourage discrimination and raise the risk of rolling back some of these civil rights accomplishments (Edelman, et al., 2015). Together, the management team finally understood and empathized with people who felt discriminated against after hearing the anecdotal stories of black Airbnb guests and reading the Harvard research paper.

The servant leader or management team's next move was to address the issue and take appropriate action. To study and assess Airbnb's design and contract/agreement model, management in this instance engaged a team of civil-rights advocates, including former US attorney general Eric Holder, the head of the ACLU's legislative offices, and numerous academics. The management then experimented with how customer profiles would be displayed and how hosts may sign up for guest reservations in an effort to lessen incidences of prejudice. Even while the new system is far from ideal, it is a positive development.

CHAPTER 5

HEALING

"Healing yourself is connected with healing others." - Yoko Ono

---

I t is absolutely natural for everyone to have some emotional baggage. People encounter both the pleasures and the sorrows of life as they go through life. While one person is enjoying the birth of a child, another is mourning the loss of a parent; while one person is celebrating a significant financial gain, another is worrying about how to put food on the table that night. This is how life ebbs and flows. Unfortunately, this will have an impact on every element of life, both public and private, regardless of how hard or how much one tries to push it away. Whatever the cause of the pain, the misery that results will have an impact on every element of our life. Regardless of the cause of the suffering, the servant leader knows they must endeavor to create a culture of healing. They approach leadership with a philosophy of service first. The servant leader is aware that for productivity to be at its highest, each team member must feel complete.

Numerous leadership theories have attempted to link a leader's management style to the results of that style on their followers (Bass & Bass, 2008). Building and maintaining connections with their followers is a key component of affiliate and coaching leadership. Affiliate leaders pay close attention to their members' emotional health. The mentoring connection required by the coaching leadership style is one of mentorship, with the goal of imparting the skills required for the work at hand. Because of the relationship, this mentoring may also include healing. Building connections between leaders and followers, organizations, and communities may help bring about this healing. Many researchers have also attempted to evaluate these presumptions. Several of these research looked at the premise that developing a supportive community environment might improve followers' well-being and emotional health (Black, 201o). According to research, followers who feel better about themselves are more devoted to and satisfied with their affiliation with the organization (Babkus et al., 2011). In general, individuals are more productive and eager to put effort into the purpose when they are content and feel encouraged.

"Servant leaders have a special orientation towards the emotional healing of followers," according to Wheeler (Wheeler, 2011). A psychologically and emotionally healthy society or workforce is created by a servant leader who demonstrates traits of empathy, compassion, and a desire to heal others. A servant leader also fosters stronger senses of unity, teamwork, and long-lasting connections among their followers, the leader, and each other while keeping the healing process in mind.

Numerous internal and external forces have an impact on a person's emotional health. Without any kind of intervention, a troubled person will have an impact on the group's or organization's long-term health. The organizational leader in this situation must "handle emotions rather than just control objective facts and statistics" (Ravinda et al., 2017). In addition to attending to the demands and objectives of the mission or organization, servant leaders also need to be considerate of and ready to handle the emotional needs of their subordinates.

The Healing Process

Everyone carries some emotional baggage; it's very natural. People go through life and encounter not just its pleasures but also its sorrows. When one person celebrates the birth of a child, another is grieving the loss of a parent; when one person enjoys a great quantity of money, another is concerned about how to prepare food that night. This is how life flows in and out. Unfortunately, no matter how much one tries to deny it or push it away, it will have an impact on every facet of life, both public and private. The ensuing pain will have an impact on every element of our life, regardless of the cause of the suffering. No matter where the pain comes from, the servant leader knows they must endeavor to create a culture of healing. They have a philosophy of service first. In order for productivity to be at its highest, the servant leader is aware that every team member must feel complete.

Many leadership theories have attempted to link a leader's leadership style to the effects that leadership has on their follo-

wers (Bass & Bass, 2008). Relationship building and mainte-
nance are crucial components of affiliate and coaching
leadership. The emotional health of their followers is a priority
for affiliate leaders. The mentorship connection required by the
coaching leadership style aims to impart the abilities required
for the work at hand, and because of the relationship, this
mentoring may also extend to healing. By focusing on developing connections between leaders and followers, organizations,
and communities, this healing may be accomplished. Additionally, several scholars have attempted to put these presumptions
to the test. The premise that developing a supportive community atmosphere might improve followers' well-being and
emotional health was the focus of many of these investigations
(Black, 2010). Researchers discovered that supporters who feel
better about themselves are more dedicated to and show higher
satisfaction with the organization to which they belong (Babkus
et al., 2011). People are often more productive and eager to work
hard toward the objective when they are content and feel
encouraged.

By having a special focus on their followers' emotional well-
being, according to Wheeler, servant leaders "have a particular
orientation" (Wheeler, 2011). A society or workforce with a
strong mental and emotional well-being is created by a servant
leader who demonstrates traits of empathy, compassion, and a
desire to cure others. In addition, a servant leader fosters greater
comradery, teamwork, and long-lasting bonds between their
followers, the leader, and one another while keeping the healing
process in mind.

An individual's mental health suffers as a result of several
internal and external stresses. Without any kind of assistance, a

disturbed person will have an impact on the long-term well-being of the group or organization. The organization's leader in this situation "must be the managers of emotions rather than the managers of merely hard facts and statistics" (Ravinda et al., 2017). In addition to attending to the demands and objectives of the mission or organization, servant leaders must also be conscientiously aware of and equipped to handle issues relating to their subordinates' emotional well-being.

CHAPTER 6
AWARENESS

"The key to growth is the introduction of higher dimensions of consciousness into our awareness." - Lao Tzu

On the surface, the concept of awareness seems to be very straightforward. In the majority of transactional models, this merely entails monitoring the status of the project in question and communicating any updates to a subsequent chain-level supervisor. Being aware is a challenging and ever-evolving process for the servant leader since it affects both the team's overall and individual emotional health in addition to the success of their task. This implies that a leader has to spend time getting to know their followers as people, not merely as gears in a machine. One of the main factors that contribute to team conflict is external pressure; a team member who is experiencing financial difficulties will bring those problems into the group. While awareness helps one see things more clearly, it also requires a leader to embrace both the positive and negative aspects of a situation and take the necessary action to increase the group's efficiency and cohesion. Three different forms of consciousness exist: self-awareness, awareness of others, and political awareness.

Internal Self-Awareness

The first stage of being fully aware starts with an awareness of self (internal self-awareness) and how others regard ourselves if the objective of awareness is to fulfill the needs of others in order to convince those being led towards a shared goal (external self-awareness). According to research, self-aware individuals tend to be more creative, confident, and self-aware. They also tend to make better judgments and communicate more effectively. People who are aware of who they are and what they need to succeed often make better employees or team members, more effective leaders, and tend to form more effective teams (Eurich, 2018).

Internal self-awareness refers to how well we grasp who we are as a person. This calls for intense self-reflection—the urge to go far inside to uncover our true selves and what we genuinely need as opposed to what we desire. Some of life's most challenging questions, in Eurich's opinion, are where the servant leader's journey to self-awareness begins (Schoff, n.d.):

- Who am I?

- Why am I here?

- Where have I been?

- Where am I going?

- How will I get there?

- What does success look like?

- What are my morals and where do I get them?

I, who? The majority of individuals play many societal positions, including that of kid, parent, aunt or uncle, grandparent, follower, or leader. The whole person is made up of all of these factors working together. A team's intended output must be considered when a leader decides who they are in each of these jobs and, more importantly, how those roles support or hinder that production. When attempting to answer the question "Who am I?," one must also consider the source of their morality, or sense of good and evil. Morality often derives from personal and social belief systems and experiences. For instance, most people agree that it is immoral to steal; our parents, teachers, or other role models teach us this lesson while we are growing up. A certain percentage of people will learn that lesson the hard way by stealing something. Where experience counts is in this situation. It is completely feasible to learn from other people's experiences even if one does not need to experience anything in order to learn from it.

Even when individuals are aware of the potential consequences of breaching moral laws, the best way to learn is typically to see failure or punishment rather than really experiencing it. It is essential to remember that morality and sense of identity are often situational and dependent on the environment or needs of the person. Even if it is unlawful to steal from a farmers' market, what if someone is in need? What if that apple will provide a starving youngster with food? Although most individuals are aware that stealing is bad, should one still be penalized in these situations? Many people will disagree, but some people will redefine morality to prohibit stealing in order to feed the needy.

How will I get there, where have I been, and where am I going? If one does not know where they have been, how can they possibly know where they are going? A servant leader has to lay out their own path toward self-awareness. The past cannot be changed, but the lessons that may be drawn from it can help someone on their journey to self-awareness. Additionally, when individuals gain self-awareness, the way in which they perceive the lessons learned in the past may alter, which will have an impact on the present and future. Think about the professional decisions individuals make when they are growing up. A person may have a childhood dream of becoming a dentist. As the kid gets older, they go to the dentist often; however, one visit results in a dental trauma, such as a root canal, and as a result, their childhood ambitions of becoming a dentist have been replaced with nightmares.

Making a plan becomes more crucial as individuals grow to understand themselves—their fears, talents, and flaws. A leader has to define their ideal selves. What type of leader does one want to be, in other words? Leaders discover their strong and weak points as they travel this path of self-awareness. A servant leader is aware of these flaws and will try to improve them through both professional and personal growth. Again, it is crucial to keep in mind that the servant leader is aware of this and works to find solutions even if they are conscious they do not have all the answers. Additionally, by having a vague sense of who they are, servant leaders may identify their own assets and identify areas for development, taking the required actions to advance. According to studies, internal self-awareness "is adversely connected to anxiety, tension, and depression; it is positively related to work and relationship satisfaction, personal and social control, and happiness" (Eurich, 2018).

External Awareness

A servant leader must not only be aware of themselves, but also be mindful of others around them and their followers. Knowing oneself also entails understanding how others see us. This has the highest priority for the servant leader. It seems to reason that followers would follow a leader who is uncertain of themselves. There is less buy-in and nothing to gain for either the leader or the followers if the followers think the leader is inept and oblivious of what is happening. The relationships between leaders and their followers are improved, they feel more fulfilled, and they are typically more successful when they are able to perceive themselves as their followers view them (Eurich, 2018).

Contrary to common opinion, a servant leader's increased self-awareness is not usually a result of experience or authority. In truth, individuals don't always take the lessons from their mistakes to heart. Unfortunately, having a lot of experience sometimes makes it harder to be conscious of oneself. Experience may generate a feeling of security that often makes it difficult to identify and eliminate misleading information. This is particularly true when a leader believes they are "extremely experienced." Many people who have a lot of expertise develop a false feeling of assurance or overconfidence that might prevent them from growing personally and blind them to the needs of their followers. A leader is also more inclined to exaggerate their own talents and abilities the more authority they have. Because a leader may believe they are smarter than their followers or because asking for input from followers may cost money, having power might make someone less eager to listen. Feedback is often given to the leader and is either fabricated or will be received with hostility or opposition.

A servant leader should constantly be aware of themselves, but this goes beyond mere self-reflection. Many individuals think that introspection—the act of focusing only on one's own actions, emotions, and thoughts—improves self-awareness. Unexpectedly, those who just focus inward "are less self-aware and report poorer work satisfaction and well-being," according to research (Eurich, 2018).

A servant leader should be self-aware, yet merely asking "why" is insufficient. Simply asking why doesn't work since individuals can't access their unconscious ideas, beliefs, emotions, or motivations. Because subconscious motivations impact so much of what individuals do, they sometimes invent explanations for situations that seem genuine but are actually false. For instance, when a person (employee) exhibits behavior that is out of character, others may assume that the employee lacks maturity and is unfit for the job while the real cause was low blood sugar.

The difficulty with asking why is that it doesn't address the topic of how mistaken someone is. Instead, the majority of individuals will dispute how certain they are that they are correct. Rarely is the human brain reasonable, and even less often is an individual's judgment bias-free. People tend to embrace what seems right and reasonable rather than what is truly right and reasonable. People accomplish all of this while denying the veracity of our illogical first "insights," as well as any contradicting facts. No matter how plausible an initial explanation may seem, the human brain with its warped memories and coerced cognition will follow it.

Last but not least, asking why is bad since it invites negative thoughts and ideas into our introspection. This is particularly true when attempting to explain an undesirable result. A student could inquire, "Why did I fail that assignment?" after earning a poor mark on one. They're likely to concentrate on an explanation based on their flaws, anxieties, and insecurities. A logical evaluation of a person's strengths and flaws should be the main objective of introspection if the goal is to become self-aware.

People should ask what or how questions as opposed to why. It is possible to concentrate on details rather than being overwhelmed by the scope of the problem by asking what and how. People are compelled to think about the processes performed objectively to identify flaws, blunders, achievements, and failures when they are asked what/how. As a result, it becomes easier to keep an eye on the future and have the confidence to make the required adjustments to ensure the project's or goal's continued success.

Starbucks CEO Kevin Johnson is "a genuine servant leader, and he will manage Starbucks as this organization embarks its next adventure," according to departing CEO Howard Schultz (Schultz, 2018). Johnson followed Schultz's example and proceeded with his forward-thinking ways of thinking. Because Schultz and Johnson worked to ensure that their staff members feel appreciated, they were able to understand that the purpose of servant leadership is to create people and communities. Starbucks provided access to healthcare coverage for both full-time and part-time employees because they were aware of the difficulties faced by the majority of low wage workers (Schultz, 2018). Starbucks trains its managers to lead with a servant's heart; instead of instructing staff on how to do a task, managers are to ask, "How can I assist you?" 2018 (Cooper). This is essential for understanding a leader's followers and vice versa. Giving instructions on how to complete a job to staff is a highly authoritarian leadership style. It built a bond when a leader inquired about how they might assist their people. In this way, it makes a follower feel included in the group and appreciate that a leader took the time to assist them.

Additionally, Starbucks goes above and above with its employee perks by giving qualifying staff members equity via their "Bean Stock" program. Employees are given a "Restricted Stock Unit (RSU)" in the form of a grant. Employees earn the second half of the RSU in the second year. The RSU reaches maturity and turns into regular stock after two years. Employees have the option to keep or share their RSU after it converts. Starbucks achieves two goals with this. Employees are first made to feel appreciated and welcomed. It offers workers a cause to stick with the firm for longer than a year or two. Second, being aware of how the business is seen by outsiders (external awareness)—providing workers with benefits shows that you value them and care about their long-term success with the business.

Political Awareness

People are sociable beings by nature. Whether at work, in their communities, at the office, or within their families, the majority of individuals want to feel like they belong. There is an adage in Hebrew that says, "There are three viewpoints wherever two individuals are present." Conflict is unavoidable because no two people are alike; they all have distinct histories, worldviews, and religious beliefs. Most of the time, individuals are aware of this and modify in order to "get along" with everyone in the group, or, more specifically, they conform to the group politics.

The whiner, the complainer, or the cheerleader—the list is as long as the group—will start to play a part in the dynamics of the groupings as people start to establish them. This is true in all contexts, from close friendships to board members of corporations. In each situation, a leader makes an effort to comprehend the dynamics of the group and tries to influence those dynamics in favor of the group as a whole and the objective at hand. This implies that a leader must delegate authority over the many components of the ultimate objective to others. The purpose of the servant leader is to inspire people to want to do better for themselves and their communities. A leader strives to help each member within the group by ensuring they have the necessary resources to achieve their full potential inside their position and beyond.

After returning to his position as CEO of Apple Inc., Steve Jobs worked with the board, customers, developers, and programmers to identify the issues that were causing Apple to continue to experience financial losses (Shontell, 2011). Jobs believed modifications were required once he understood the dynamics governing the present Apple product line and development. His first action was to cancel Newton, a pricey project that was draining the business of money. In addition, he reviewed Apple's large product portfolio, removing the majority of what he considered to be poor initiatives and focusing on personal and professional desktop and personal computing. Jobs was able to more effectively manage the company's resources by streamlining Apple's product range. When he partnered up with Microsoft in 1997, he listened to computer specialists and formed alliances that were advantageous to both sides (Shontell, 2011). In the end, Jobs was able to navigate the politics of the tech industry and utilized his servant leadership abilities to leave the profession in better shape.

Politics, according to Crick (1993), is the process of rallying support for a viewpoint, choice, or course of action in which "people work together through institutionalized procedures to resolve differences, to conciliate different interests and values, and to make public policies in the pursuit of common goals" (Crick, 2004). Understanding the beliefs and motives of one's followers is what the servant leader implies by having political awareness. Everybody brings a unique set of experiences and ideals to the table. It is important for servant leaders to comprehend how these experiences change followers' attitudes, mindsets, and beliefs. A leader is better equipped to manage group discussions and create agreement among all stakeholders when they are aware of this. The "difference between someone who can't get an idea off the ground and accepted in an organization and someone who can" is how several academics define political awareness (Bacharach, 2005).

CHAPTER 7
PERSUASION

"Persuasion is achieved by the speaker's personal character when the speech is so spoken as to make us think him credible. We believe good men more fully and more readily than others: this is true generally whatever the question is, and absolutely true where exact certainty is impossible and opinions are divided." - Aristotle

---

Leadership by persuasion is often forced by threat and intimidation under the authoritarian, pacesetting, and laissez-faire paradigms. The ultimate result is always the main concern for the leader; either their followers can fill the jobs they are selected for, or someone else can. All decisions are decided by the leader under pacesetting and authoritarian models, with little to no input from others. While this paradigm is a good method to coordinate outcomes, it is not sustainable in terms of development and progress for both individuals and groups. This strategy saps followers' or workers' drive to better themselves or their productivity by making them feel cut off from the overall objective. While the outcome is crucial, so are personal development and the environment of the group. In general, followers who feel heard, respected, and like they belong are happier and more effective.

The transactional approach is unsustainable, as the servant leadership paradigm recognizes. People start to lose interest in the organization or the cause once they stop feeling respected. The servant leader strives to make sure that each team member feels appreciated in order to achieve this. The servant leader tries to foster agreement among their team members in order to achieve this. To ensure that each colleague has a say in the decision-making process, they attempt to build an understanding among teammates. This is done to influence people to desire to work toward improving themselves, which enhances the team or community as a whole.

Constantly keep in mind that persuasion differs from compulsion. A leader who is serving to persuade understands that they must persuade everyone in the group to concur to work together toward a shared objective. A good leader never bullies or threatens their people into obedience. A group leader does not overlook or minimize individuals who are struggling. A leader works with their followers to help them develop and helps to create possibilities to better their followers' life and the group's intended goal. A leader tries to convince everyone in the group to share a same purpose or vision. Due of this, a lot of organizations adopt a mission or vision statement. It is a straightforward declaration that establishes a shared understanding or expectations for all group members.

All organization members and the general public have their queries answered by the mission statement. An organization might decide to adopt a mission or vision statement along the lines of "To always conduct ourselves with tolerance and integrity; displaying empathy, care, and concern for our clients in a transparent no-pressure sales environment in order to provide an unparalleled positive [service]," for instance. (Bbl, 2015). In this case, it is expected that every member of the group would conduct themselves in accordance with the code, acting with respect and honesty (true active listening), demonstrating empathy (understanding), and caring (a desire to serve) for their customers' needs. A set of values that apply to all members is also included in the mission statement.

The goal of a servant leader is to inspire their team members to perform at their highest level and try to accomplish more in practically every situation. This is what everyone in the group ought to ideally want, but we do not live in a perfect world. There will be instances when one or more team members fall short of expectations in practically every team. A lack of training or an outside factor—such as a dispute with a spouse or money problems—that the team is unaware of may be to blame. In the past, a low-performing employee would often get counseling, a possible reminder of the expectations, or be fired and replaced with someone else. In other words, the danger of losing their job compels a person to work more.

This strategy is rejected by the servant leader paradigm. In order to motivate employees, threats and intimidation are ineffective strategies. A servant leader collaborates with their followers to identify the issues that the team or followers are facing. Before removing a team member from the group, a leader must take the time to get to know their followers and understand their motives in order to eliminate any obstacles that may be impeding the team's progress. The majority of the time, the issues are structural: inadequate training, murky expectations, and frequent changes without warning. All of these problems are ones that the employee or follower cannot manage. It is the responsibility of a servant leader to first grasp the situation before taking action rather than the other way around.

A leader's mission is to develop others' trust and motivate them to take better care of themselves and their communities by using their persuasive abilities. This is a unique ability that servant leaders always strive to improve. A leader must create an environment that encourages lines of open and honest communication as well as a feeling of trust and integrity in order to urge people to take action. A leader must leave the workplace to develop a personal relationship with their followers in order to do this. Make an effort to get to know them; show empathy for their problems and way of life; share in their successes; and provide support when necessary. Serving others and encouraging others to improve themselves are the foundation of the servant leader's life. A servant leader instills a sense of belonging among their followers, making them feel like family.

American billionaire Warren Buffett said that trust is the most crucial component of any company (Schwantes, 2020). Buffett played a crucial role in the situation and had the capacity to motivate others. The discrepancy between what individuals promise to do and what they really do, or the "say-do" gap, is what Buffet refers to (Schwantes, 2020). He also highlights the need for a leader to create a climate of trust so that followers feel free to take chances that will benefit both them and their team. Failure is a common fear, yet taking risks entails some failure. Building trust begins with the knowledge that they are supported through both their accomplishments and disappointments.

Buffett had amassed an incredible fortune of well over $65 billion by the time he was 85 years old (Business Day, 2016). In 2010, Buffett established The Giving Pledge after switching his focus from accumulating wealth to charitable endeavors. This charitable organization's goal is to support charities by persuading the world's wealthiest individuals to pledge to devote more than half of their lifetime fortunes to charitable causes. This is a problem for most individuals; for billionaires, it is more challenging since every financial decision is always being scrutinized.

Buffett spoke about how he was able to leverage his position and standing to urge others to give during an interview with "60 Minutes." Buffett first used a technique known as backward planning, or mapping. He started to put together the steps required to complete his task with the ultimate result as his main focus. Admitting a leader's weakness is the first step in convincing others to assist. In Buffett's instance, he was aware that his own organizational capabilities could not keep up with managing a massive worldwide business. Recognizing this weakness, Buffett sought out Bill and Melinda Gates, whose Bill & Melinda Gates Foundation had a track record of developing organizational abilities (Business Day, 2016).

Then Buffett contacted the people he was appealing to for donations. He made an effort to fully comprehend their viewpoints while paying attention to their worries and wishes. He learned what was most important to them. In light of this, Buffett decided to concentrate his organization's efforts on fundraising rather than establishing stringent guidelines for how donations would be handled (Business Day, 2016). Buffett was able to attract additional billionaires to join his organization by offering stakeholders a role in the decision-making process and enabling contributors to choose the causes they considered to be in need.

The Giving Pledge continues to support its members by addressing their fears through an ongoing series of workshops, forums, and training sessions in order to help them find risk-free methods of giving money. The Giving Pledge is aware that making a pledge to donate billions of dollars to charity carries risks. Additionally, Buffett makes sure that he fulfills his obligations to others and continues to support charity organizations. He has contributed over $36 billion in Berkshire Hathaway shares to the The Giving Pledge project (Stempel, 2020).

By providing each member a feeling of power, Buffett listened to his followers, encouraged their particular pursuits, and included them in the decision-making process. To provide his group members access to resources, he created a support system. Finally, he built trust among the group members by acknowledging his flaws and creating an organization with specialists to handle them. Others are persuaded to join by the organization itself and his dedication to it; he utilized his position of power and influence to inculcate in its members a feeling of integrity and honesty that, in the organization's aspirations, would encourage others to join.

CHAPTER 8
CONCEPTUALIZATION AND FORESIGHT

"Success is about dedication. You may not be where you want to be or do what you want to do when you're on the journey. But you've got to be willing to have vision and foresight that leads you to an incredible end." - Usher

---

Leaders are visionaries. A desire to take a concept and transform it into something real and effective is at the core of every leader's motivation. While the majority of leaders are excellent at developing broad ideas and concepts, putting those ideas into action is often a completely different story. A notion or vision of what they see their project to be is often created by leaders. It may be a good or a service, but it's harder to make that notion a reality. Many CEOs find that the day-to-day responsibilities of running a business cause their thoughts or visions to stagnate.

Any transactional leadership approach (authoritarian, pace-setting, laissez-faire) places the group leader at the center of operations, coordinating activities, making decisions, micromanaging the actions of their followers, and leading their team in a vacuum—having eliminated all other voices. These approaches do have certain benefits; concentrating control and coordinating from a single place has its appeal and could increase an organization's productivity.

Servant leaders have large dreams, but they also work to develop their capacity for having big dreams. The servant leader goes beyond the ordinary circumstances in order to accomplish this. An effective servant leader may approach a situation, group, or concept from the goal—the final outcome—point of view. The servant leader model emphasizes on letting the leader concentrate on directing the group's overall course, as opposed to conventional leadership models that encourage leaders to prioritize short-term objectives. This calls for focus and repetition.

Conceptualization is often left to the board of directors in a major company, as it should be because they are the organization's leaders. Regrettably, experience has shown what boards may develop into in the regular business operations of the corporation. The firm was on the brink of bankruptcy when Apple Inc. requested Steve Jobs to take it again (Shontell, 2011). As investor discontent increased, the board started to investigate why Apple was losing money. They started probing deeply into the Apple business, looking at everything from the goods to the supply chain to the employees. In other words, the board did not lead the business into a more lucrative position; rather, it pushed itself down in the daily operations. While the servant leader should be concerned with certain everyday challenges, they also need to strike a balance. Instead of tackling the issue head-on, leaders should provide their people with the tools they need to resolve it.

The technique of persuasive mapping is one that many leadership paradigms use. This is not really a novel idea; education departments at universities throughout the world have been teaching this methodology for years. Grant Wiggins first offered the "Backward Design" lesson preparation concept in the publication Understanding by Design (ASCD, 2005). The intention was to assist instructors in creating stronger, more in-depth unit learning plans without becoming bogged down in the minute particulars. No of the circumstance, the servant-leader is a teacher. Servant leaders try to uplift people by offering advice, assistance, or instruction to inspire them to seek better outcomes for themselves and their communities. Putting ideas into practice requires preparation, whether in business or education.

The servant leader paradigm starts by asking why, as opposed to how, before commencing the planning process. The planning process is forced to concentrate on the outcome by asking why. Big ideas and concepts may be found in why questions; this is what motivates the group. It is the group's vision and purpose. These are the broad ideas that students are expected to understand; in the field of education, they are referred to as learning objectives. For instance, a math instructor may designate as a learning objective that pupils will recognize and comprehend basic equations. The instructor anticipates that the pupils will have learned this learning objective at the conclusion of the course. The idea behind why a firm exists in the first place in terms of business. The why is the outcome of the group's activity when considering community organizing.

The next logical step is figuring out how to fulfill the goal's requirements after the why issue has been resolved. Here, a teacher thinks about the "pieces" of the whole as part of the backward planning process. They choose the components that are necessary to fulfill the learning objective. A teacher may divide a lesson into addition, subtraction, multiplication, and division if the learning objective is for the pupils to comprehend and recognize basic equations. The groundwork for achieving the why is provided by those four issues. A teacher may then use that information to locate the materials required for their pupils to achieve the learning objective.

This same kind of mapping is used by servant leaders, much as by instructors. As the head of a company, you already have some kind of ultimate objective in mind. We've previously identified the fundamental reason why. Like a teacher, a servant leader reorients their attention to how to fulfill and exceed the requirements of the final project. All interested parties participate in this brainstorming process. The leader motivates their followers to take ownership in the organization and the defined objectives by forging consensus and including everyone in the decision-making process.

In 1967, Herb Kelleher helped co-found what would eventually become Southwest Airlines (Shine, 2019), with the intention of democratizing air travel at a time when it was too costly for most families. Few big airlines now dominate the majority of the global air transport business, with other carriers stumbling about on the periphery. He believed that the industry's main issue was that the airline sector was subject to onerous and oppressive regulations, which increased the expense of travel. Kelleher made a significant effort to urge Congress to de-regulate the airline business after achieving that goal in 1978. (How Herb Kelleher Made the World a Whole Lot Smaller, 2019).

Kelleher started to assemble the elements of his aim and seek the aid of others with the overall goal of lowering the cost of air travel and making it accessible to the general public. Making his staff feel important and valued members of the organization was one of the first basic questions Kelleher had to address. He desired their enthusiasm and happiness when they reported for duty. Along with his business partner Rollin King, Kelleher started giving his staff bonuses, greater pay, better insurance, tuition reimbursements, and even free flights. Workers that are content are productive employees. Kelleher maintained an open door policy while serving as the company's CEO and often left the building to speak with lower-level staff members. Kelleher essentially changed the "customer first" business strategy to a "employee first" business model. Kelleher made sure that the day-to-day aspects felt his touch even if he may have delegated authority for each part of the organization to others.

The next stage in providing affordable air travel was to find ways to reduce expenses while keeping employee wages the same. Kelleher developed the concept of a no-frills airline by removing luxuries like in-flight meals and movies in favor of peanuts and soft drinks after researching the market and recognizing the costs involved with the sector. Instead of broadening the company fleet, Southwest chose the Boeing 737 and examined the airframe to determine how many people could fly in comfort and safety. Their methodology also did away with the distinction between "classes" in air travel, such as first-class and economy. Instead, by making all tickets the same price, they were able to simplify their pricing approach. Kelleher flew into airports like Chicago Midway rather than Chicago O'Hare to avoid paying astronomical gate fees by using smaller, secondary, and regional airports. Kelleher also used a "point-to-point" flying concept as opposed to a hub and spoke strategy to save costs. Southwestern employs a system akin to a bus route rather than flying back and forth via a central hub (Labich & Hadjian, 2020).

A leader must not only be able to envision and think creatively, but they must also be able to exercise foresight. "A trait that allows the servant leader to grasp the lessons from the past, realities of the present, and the possible ramifications of a choice for the future" is what foresight is defined as (Spears, n.d.). To do this, a leader must possess the capacity to draw lessons from the past and correct errors by applying those lessons to the current situation. In order to ascertain any potential negative or positive consequences, they should also consider the future. Though conception and foresight are relatively different, to the servant leader, one goes hand in hand with the other. A leader must think about the possible benefits of the project as they develop an idea and define their objectives, which includes answering the why questions "what is the aim or goal?" Although finishing a project successfully is obviously the main objective, how will that project be beneficial in the long run?

A servant leader is a lifelong learner. A leader has to keep taking stock of the past and the lessons acquired. A leader then has to be able to adapt those teachings to the circumstances at hand. A leader must draw on the experiences of others as well since nothing occurs in a vacuum, even if study and introspection are important in this endeavor. Various individuals have different experiences. Through the process of acquiring resources, this is included into the backward planning paradigm. The servant leader is aware of the importance of their followers as resources for completing the current task. A leader may utilize their followers' and their own experiences to guide the company by getting to know them and developing an empathy for them. Again, a servant leader steps back by enabling their followers to speak openly about their experiences and including them in decision-making. By doing this, a leader may gain the support of their followers while also integrating their opinions into the organization's preparation for possible issues or future developments (foresight).

Warren Buffett spoke about utilizing a persuasive, or reverse, mapping to set up and grow the organization when he spoke about the formation of The Giving Pledge (Business Day, 2016). Building a coalition of affluent people who all agreed to devote half of their lifetime fortunes to charity organizations was the idea, or main objective, of the organization. Buffett asked people he was seeking to donate to The Giving Pledge for advise before starting this project. Buffett has always guided The Giving Pledge by drawing on the experiences of others. Bill and Melinda Gates were engaged by Buffett to take care of the organizational demands while he concentrated on forming his coalition. Buffett leveraged their knowledge of running their own Bill & Melinda Gates Foundation to assist establish and expand The Giving Pledge. Buffett overcame administrative challenges that might have hampered the development of The Giving Pledge by bringing the Gates on early.

Buffett sought out prospective partners to hear about their charitable giving experiences in light of his own. It is advantageous to draw on the experiences of others when forming a team or group when deciding where or how to lead the group. What could be helpful to one individual may be a barrier to another. Through his conversations, Buffett discovered that many billionaires were eager to donate half of their wealth, but that doing so would be fraught with legal complications and worries about stringent regulations that would limit what qualifies as "charity" (Business Day, 2016). After gaining these insights, Buffett returned to his core business with the wisdom to alter his concept. Rather thxan concentrating on a traditional charity— choosing which causes to support—Buffett changed his focus to assisting others in learning how to donate money rather than setting up a conventional trust. By putting this change in thinking into practice, Buffett was able to meet the demands of his followers and provide them the tools they needed to properly support their charitable endeavors.

CHAPTER 9
STEWARDSHIP

"Sustainable development is the pathway to the future we want for all. It offers a framework to generate economic growth, achieve social justice, exercise environmental stewardship and strengthen governance." - Ban Ki-moon

The term "stewardship" is derived from the word "steward," which is used to define someone who takes care of objects, people, events, processes, etc. Stewardship is the capacity to keep something in trust for another, according to author Peter Block's 1993 book Stewardship and The Empowered Manager. In other words, the servant leader must ensure that their teams, businesses, and initiatives serve society as a whole. If a servant leader's main objective is to serve their followers, then it stands to reason that their organizations should help society as a whole.

At its core, servant leadership is about taking care of others. Stewardship, in the eyes of the servant leader, is all about advancing the welfare of each individual within a team or company (Churchill et al., 2015). Servant leaders care more and exercise less control in this way. As essential as the objective itself is, the servant leader places equal value on the welfare of their followers and inspires them to strive for greater goals for themselves by taking responsibility for their professional and personal growth. The project objective and the measures required to attain it are the leader's top priorities in an authoritarian leadership approach. If the leader's main concern is the outcome, then the leader must also take on project control. This leadership approach is conducive to micromanaging group members. On the other side, a laissez-faire or hands-off attitude causes alienation and confusion among followers.

The goal of the servant leader is to strike a balance between fostering the professional and personal growth of their followers and maintaining the momentum of the current purpose. The adoption of this stewardship model by major tech companies like Google, Microsoft, and Apple has just lately occurred. Companies like Google have put in place strict internship programs that combine young Google recruit teams with seasoned engineers and developers. The experienced team members serve as team leads and give assistance and resources as required when the organization adopts a servant leadership model. Team members are able to take responsibility of their job and their expertise thanks to this "guide on the side" strategy while still acting as resources and motivators. Final outcomes are driven by the servant leader, but the team is given flexibility and assistance as required to decide how to get there. A leader also shows genuine concern and compassion for their followers by accepting responsibility for helping them flourish. This individual effort on the part of a leader fosters a feeling of community among followers as well as a desire to grow for the benefit of the team.

A leader must continuously assess and reassess the organization's progress toward the goal and make adjustments as needed in order to retain stewardship of the company. A leader must also have the vision to see trends and patterns that can enhance progress while avoiding typical mistakes and foreseeing possible roadblocks to success. This requires the servant leader to use their own judgment in addition to advice from colleagues and other specialists. The servant leader distributes the team's success—or failure—among all members by reflecting inside and including others in the decision-making process. Teams, leaders, and followers are motivated to perform better and go above and beyond the requirements of the end result by this shared responsibility.

This entails providing continuous education and providing incentives for it in many organizations. Doctors and nurses in the healthcare sector are required to stay up to date on patient care and treatment. Many healthcare organizations provide their staff members with tuition reimbursement so they may pursue their education as science advances and new, more effective, and better therapeutic techniques are found. Employees are urged to take advantage of internal training opportunities given by many IT organizations, including Google. Many businesses also provide their staff members the freedom and encouragement to follow their own hobbies while still contributing to the team.

Encouragement of self-improvement increases the likelihood that followers will utilize their newly discovered talents and interests for the benefit of the group as a whole. Additionally, followers tend to be happier and more eager to give more of themselves to the team and the larger cause when they feel that their leaders have a real interest in them as people.

Developing leaders from inside is another strategy servant leaders use to maintain stewardship of the business as a whole. A leader must give others—their followers—the opportunity to identify their strengths and flaws for this to occur. Leaders may help their followers develop their abilities and become into servant leaders in their own right by giving them opportunity to capitalize on their strengths and correct their flaws. Many businesses have created their own leadership development programs based on this approach, combining the organization's goal and vision as well as imparting the knowledge and abilities required to guide the business into the future. Well-rounded leadership programs are developed and implemented by organizations to maintain the group's path. Leaders also leave a legacy of information, abilities, and wisdom that may be handed from one generation of leaders to the next. Future leaders might be guided and pushed to create fresh and original solutions or ideas by a leader who imparts the lessons acquired from prior events.

Maintaining the idea and direction of the vision is one of the top concerns in the majority of blue-chip enterprises. A leader carefully creates the organization's goal and vision and sets it on a successful course. In an authoritarian or autocratic style of leadership, the leader is completely responsible for the organization's triumphs and failures. Although this strategy is more effective at achieving short-term objectives, it also places the burden of the organization's legacy entirely on the shoulders of the leader. According to the servant-leadership paradigm, meeting the needs of others should be a leader's first priority. A servant leader makes sure their legacy will endure long after they are gone by accepting stewardship in the service of the skills and aspirations of others. The servant leader secures the legacy of their business by establishing a leadership program and developing future leaders from within. A good leader should be able to communicate their ideas and vision while giving their followers the freedom to influence the direction of the business and contribute to its legacy. Many businesses that use a servant leadership approach outlive those that use a conventional, top-down approach. Future leaders are developed at companies like Amazon via a meticulously groomed and planned training program that instills the company's beliefs and aims in each team member, from the upper management team to the employees in the fulfillment facilities.

When Google was founded in September 1998, Larry Page and Sergey Brin had an idea for a way to search and index the World Wide Web that would later turn out to be quite successful (Fitz-patrick, 2014). When Google first started, the goal was to create the best search engine in the world, allowing consumers to access material on the internet that is freely accessible in a practical way that is fast, simple, and accurate. In order to do this, Page and Brin embarked on a search for financiers, artists, and programmers who shared their goals (persuasion/backward planning). By meeting their workers' needs and encouraging their innovation as the business expanded, Page and Brin upended the IT industry. Many people used to believe that computer businesses recruited designers and programmers who spent their days writing code in isolated offices; however, Google was different. Co-founder of Twitter Biz Stone said of Google that it was "strange place—like a crazy child country. There were these large, vibrant, bouncy balls there, but the employees were adults (Fisher, 2018). "Google could make the argument; Oh, don't worry, this is going to feel a lot like when you were a researcher. You're still an academic, you just work at Google now," said Sean Parker, the creator of Napster, who lauded Google for being able to attract brilliant engineers. 2018 (Fisher).

As the dominant search engine that is publicly accessible, Google started to broaden its software offerings outside Google Search. Page and Brin looked inside to extend their product offerings since they already adhered to the servant leadership concept. Google's team was given ownership of the company's future by instilling the purpose, vision, and values of the organization in them from the beginning. Additionally, as Google grew, Page and Brin were able to put leaders in charge of new areas while adjusting and expanding the company's original concept by implementing a servant leader mentality throughout the entire organization, creating an internal leadership program to teach staff how to be servant leaders in their own right, and enforcing the company's values and mission. Google's software product line has grown to include email, productivity/work tools, language translation, maps and navigation, cloud storage, as well as music and video hosting services in addition to its search engine. Additionally, Google has assumed the initiative in the creation of the Android and Chrome operating systems.

More recently, Google introduced the Nexus and Pixel mobile phones, the Google Home smart speaker, and Google Wifi: a mesh wireless router, further solidifying their position as a leader in the digital industry. They also entered the hardware market and the artificial intelligence industries.

CHAPTER 10
COMMITMENT TO GROWTH OF PEOPLE AND COMMUNITY

"To maintain a joyful family requires much from both the parents and the children. Each member of the family has to become, in a special way, the servant of the others." - Pope John Paul II

Servant leadership presupposes first and foremost a commitment to servicing the needs of others," Larry Spears said (Spears, 2019). The purpose or the outcome is the leader's single fundamental commitment under a typical authoritarian approach. Although some leaders may show interest in their followers, this is often transactional and may not always be distributed fairly across team members. In this situation, the leader is mainly concerned with individuals who can help him or her directly. This is when a leader favors certain people over others, to put it simply. Those who are not in the leader's good graces have a sense of detachment and lose motivation as a result.

On the other hand, same outcomes may be attained with a more laissez-faire or hands-off attitude. In this situation, the leader has relatively little influence on the individuals responsible for carrying out a project's phases or the steps themselves. The outcome of a non-existent leader is no better than that of an authoritarian, domineering leader. The hands-off leader abandons their subordinates, in contrast to an authoritarian leader who micromanages them. The idea for the project or company may have been developed by a leader, but a leader requires followers (workers) to carry it through. Followers soon lose their responsibilities and their leader when their leader abandons them and expects them to work things out on their own.

The servant leader approach aims to strike a healthy balance between showing dedication to their followers and the larger community. According to this paradigm, a leader is dedicated to the development of their followers, and this dedication is subsequently returned. The followers of a servant leader who thinks that their followers' development comes first and foremost must care about the advancement of their leader and their company. A leader who is dedicated to the development of their followers, and therefore, of their communities, develops a strong emotional connection with both. A servant leader thinks that local communities, not big organizations or governments, should be the major factors shaping people's lives (Commitment Staff, 2020).

A servant leader thinks that communities and followers both benefit from local growth. A leader must be sensitive to the requirements of the community as a whole in order for this to happen, in addition to the needs of their followers. Because of this, it's crucial for a servant leader to build strong relationships with their communities and followers. In social professions like teaching or social work, this is evident. This is compounded in other disciplines, particularly in commercial enterprise, by the demands of the firm and other elements like geography and local socioeconomic conditions. Communities, like individuals, have various standards of behavior based on their needs and surroundings. The demands of a wealthy suburb are quite different from those of an impoverished inner-city neighborhood.

It is the same thing to show a commitment to the development of both communities and people. A leader must pay attention to the community they are in just as they must listen to and get to know their followers in order to be a good leader. A leader actively listens to their followers or workers in a team or office environment. Team members are encouraged to discuss their thoughts and problems with the group and, more especially, the leader, when the listening is pertinent to the current objective. A leader takes these recommendations, attempts to put them into practice as necessary, or whatever problems they may be experiencing, and strives to resolve them. It is not sufficient to only listen to followers' opinions about the workplace. A leader that cares about others will listen to whatever a follower says and take steps to ease or even celebrate whatever they are experiencing. A young girl at a tiny American high school approached her instructor for advice on an issue; she was 17 and pregnant. She approached this instructor because she was certain they were a real servant leader who cared about both their pupils and their subject matter. In past years, the instructor attended a student's sporting events, accompanied them to dances, and attended extracurricular activities like the parent's burial or a student's performance in a church Christmas production. In order to foster a family-like environment both within and outside of the classroom, the instructor showed a genuine interest in and listened to their pupils. When the instructor gave birth, this student requested if they might adopt the kid. In this case, the teacher's reputation for servant leadership led to students entrusting them with their own kid in order to further their education. By the way, the pregnant student finished school and is now a teacher in her own classroom.

It's critical to surround oneself with individuals who share one's commitment to growth—of oneself, others, and the community. This is particularly crucial when starting a new initiative or business. Kim Savage, the executive director of HOPE International, talks on the significance of choosing employees who share your values or have a track record of becoming servant leaders. You should "start with two or three like-minded individuals who already have some innate talent or predisposition toward servant leadership," advises Savage. If you can identify a small number of servant leaders and showcase their accomplishments, you may start to convince people who are initially more hesitant to ultimately join the cause (Gibbons, 2019). Similar minds tend to feed off one another, which may be a good or bad thing. The servant leader should find this to be a fruitful experience. The circle of service will naturally spread if a servant leader is dedicated to developing others' capacities and talents. The commitment to development increases exponentially as the servant leader's influence spreads and involves a growing number of individuals, much as how followers are taught to be servant leaders.

Chick-fil-A is a wonderful example of servant leadership in action because of its dedication to both its customers and the community. Chick-fil-A was a pioneer in the servant leadership movement, putting many of its tenets into practice years before the theory was ever conceived. Three values have been ingrained in Chick-fil-culture. A's Chick-fil-A follows Savage's suggestions and hires individuals based on their character, competence, and chemistry. Second, the business promotes an environment of integrity and decency. The creator of Chick-fil-A, S. Truett Cathy, thought that building a culture of trust and showing workers that a leader appreciates them required being open and honest with them about their performance and future (Servant Leadership in Action: Two Great Examples/Infosurv, 2017). Last but not least, Chick-fil-A shares this culture with its patrons by devoting the same amount of attention to their cuisine as they do to their staff. Due to its expansion, Chick-fil-A has earned a reputation for serving up delectable food and valuing its relationships with customers and staff equally (Servant Leadership in Action: Two Great Examples/Infosurv, 2017).

Going above and beyond the scope of the organization's core goal is what it means to be a servant leader. A community is, by definition, a group of people who get along because they have similar values, aspirations, and interests. Ideally, when a group gets together to create a common plan, everyone engaged has the same objective in mind, even if they have different strategies for getting there. The mission of a servant leader's organization should be to strengthen the communities in which they operate. A servant leader broadens their circle of influence by committing to the development of the community at large, even when these activities may not directly benefit the company.

Through a variety of activities, many groups that aren't techni-cally community organizations do this. One of the best internal steps toward fostering community is allowing all members to be heard and valued. Additionally, encouraging a sense of family, self-improvement, and supporting one's physical and emotional well-being all help to build community within an organization.

The environment outside of the organization is somewhat diffe-rent and presents difficulties along the way. This is when the commitment of a servant leader to active listening and aware-ness is put to use. In comparison to community building, organi-zation building is simple. Small groups of like-minded people are naturally suited to expand with the right amount of work and assistance from everyone involved. Many people struggle to handle the level of knowledge and dedication required to build a community. A leader who is creating a community must pay attention to the needs and experiences of the people they are leading. When working in communities that are different from the leader's own, this is especially crucial. The servant leader must take a step back and recognize that their experiences are different from those of the people they serve. Many people find it challenging to develop self-awareness because doing so requires them to consider any advantages or privileges they may have had over others. On the other hand, some may need to acknowledge how challenging their prior experiences really were. In this situation, the servant leader must first take care of themselves in order to start creating a community.

A sense of political awareness is necessary for establishing community. According to this definition, political awareness entails comprehending the context of a situation or decision from various angles and taking into account how that situation or decision will ultimately affect the community (and environment). For this reason, navigating a complicated web of opportunities and interests is a soft skill necessary to advance or improve the organization or community. Political ignorance can have serious repercussions. Former Shell UK board member Sir David Varney warns of the perils of a lack of political awareness. "Our mistake was that we were too arrogant," said Shell UK when it made the decision to decommission a sizable oil storage and loading bay along the North Sea coast in 1992. No, it was our lack of communication with and failure to foresee the concerns of our community that was to blame, not our actions (Hartley & Branick, 2006). Protests organized by environmental organizations spread like wildfire across the globe. Consumers started to boycott Shell, which caused their profits to fall. Shell ultimately changed its mind about closing the plant, but the damage had already been done. Varney viewed this circumstance as a turning point that compelled him to consider how businesses interact with their political environments.

Servant leaders communicate with their team and are aware of how their organization affects the larger community. Building community need not necessarily entail creating something distinct from an organization's brand. Global personal care product manufacturer Unilever introduced their "Real Beauty" campaign through the Dove product line in 2004. (Announcing the Dove Real Beauty Pledge, 2017). The aim of this movement was to champion "real women" and broaden the definition of beauty beyond the realm of the physically attractive. Additionally, Dove wanted to change the world's traditional exclusivity of white women by extending the definition of beauty to encompass women of all shapes, sizes, and colors.

Dove established the "Real Beauty Pledge" to strengthen their sense of community. Making a commitment is one thing; actually keeping it is another. Dove started by altering their marketing initiatives. Dove claims that since the beginning of the campaign, "real" women have been featured in their advertisements rather than using well-known models (Announcing the Dove Real Beauty Pledge, 2017). They also agreed to include women of different ages, ethnicities, sizes, skin tones, hair colors, etc. to reflect the diversity of their markets. Second, Dove promised to only show women as they actually are. Dove made the decision not to alter or falsify the images of the women used in their advertising campaign. They went one step further and made sure that the women featured in any image used gave their consent. Finally, Dove began working with "world-renowned body image experts and top universities to develop evidence-based and academically validated educational tools" as part of the Dove Self-Esteem project (The Dove Real Beauty Pledge, 2017). By providing free resources to parents and schools, they set out to educate over 20 million young people about body confidence and self-esteem (Dove Self-Esteem Project, 2020).

Although Unilever changed the Dove line's focus, positively affecting the community does not always entail organizational change or a change in philosophy. Community service is encouraged by many organizations for their members. For instance, UnitedHealth Group encourages and supports the extracurricular activities of its employees. In order to achieve this, they match employee charitable contributions and give workers the opportunity to receive a $500 grant for charity for every 30 hours of volunteer work. Over the course of time, UnitedHealth Group has contributed 2.6 million volunteer hours to over 19,000 charities (United for Giving, 2016).

While encouraging volunteerism is one way to foster a sense of community, many organizations favor a more hands-on approach. Tech companies are especially prone to this. STEM (Science, Technology, Engineering, and Math) events are frequently held in schools from primary grades through colleges around the world by Intel, Google, Apple, and other tech companies. Building community involves getting actively involved in it beyond the scope of an organization's concept. Servant leaders (and, consequently, organizations) ensure their ongoing success by fostering community. A servant leader will receive support from their community if they support it.

CHAPTER 11

SERVANT LEADERSHIP IN THE 21ST CENTURY

"The number one benefit of information technology is that it empowers people to do what they want to do. It lets people be creative. It lets people be productive. It lets people learn things they didn't think they could learn before, and so in a sense it is all about potential." - Steve Ballmer

Thousands of years have passed since the first examples of servant leadership were recorded. Academics and academics have hypothesized that Lao Tzu's works, which date back approximately 2,500 years, are where the concepts of servant leadership first started to coalesce (Valeri, 2007). His statements are widely used by leadership scholars and servant leadership proponents as a starting point justification for the evolution of this approach. A leader is ideal when others hardly realize they exist, according to Lao Tzu, who published Tao Te Ching, often known as "Old Master," over 400 years ago. Not good when people follow and praise him, and worse when they are afraid of him. "Fail to respect people, and they will fail to honor you. But a good leader, who speaks little, will have them all saying, 'We accomplished this ourselves,' when his labor is over and his goal achieved. 1995's Spears.

Tao Te Ching, often known as "The Classic Book of Integrity and the Way," is more clearly comprehended by academics and scholars when read in context. (Mair, 1990). One may see the beginning of the servant leadership style in this remark, despite the fact that there are several interpretations of it. The first thing Lao Tzu says is that a leader shouldn't be loud and micromanage; instead of seeking respect and support, a leader should respect and help their subordinates. Lao Tzu concludes by suggesting that a wise leader is one who pursues the exaltation of everyone rather than self-glorification. The philosopher Lao Tzu was neither a politician, merchant, or soldier. His writings on the practices of what would be referred to as servant leadership did not arise from a desire to create anything or operate more effectively. Lao Tzu was a servant leader in the purest sense; his job was only to impart leadership knowledge to upcoming leaders.

Lao Tzu's ideas on servant leadership were not unique. Examples of servant leadership have often been seen throughout history. A leader should be prepared to serve their people selflessly, according to Cicero, who advocated this idea in ancient Rome. He spoke on the value of trusteeship (stewardship) for the individual, the group, the business or organization, and the local community. Later, in his essay "Men in Great Place," Francis Bacon (1561-1626) said that "Men in Great Place are threefold servants: servants of the sovereign or state, servants of renown, and slaves of business" (Bacon, n.d.). A leader must logically be serving others if they have no autonomy over their activities, no control over their time, and no autonomy over their personalities.

Academics in the field of leadership studies are just recently beginning to study the use of the servant leadership concept in corporate or nonreligious/political groups. In his work, Servant Leadership: A Journey Into the Nature of Legitimate Power and Greatness, researcher Robert Greenleaf first explored how the servant leadership concept may be used outside of philosophy and government (Valeri, 2007). With his definition and guiding principles, Greenleaf sought to define and characterize the qualities of a servant leader and then establish how to effectively put those qualities into practice.

The idea of servant leadership has existed throughout history. Servant leaders have always existed, from Lao Tzu to politicians and community activists. Their want to serve is powerful and, by its very nature, intensifies under the appropriate circumstances. Not that servant leadership is the "be all end all" of management and leadership—it just isn't.

Being conscious of oneself, other people, and one's surroundings is one of the fundamentals of servant leadership. Awareness of one's own strengths and limitations comes from this feeling of awareness. Additionally, it enables a leader to be aware of the assets and liabilities of those under their control as well as the society in which they live. In light of this, a servant leader's motivation is to help others develop their strengths and overcome their deficiencies. People's organizations and surrounding communities will inevitably improve as they start to better themselves.

The environment is dynamic. What is commonplace now can be seen as outdated or hazardous tomorrow. Think about how manufacturing has changed. A more transactional or authoritarian paradigm was seen as typical throughout the Industrial Revolution. There was no opportunity for progress since followers were employed for a particular task. The manager/leader was in charge of making decisions, micromanaging the workforce, and pushing for higher output levels rather than personal development.

The industrial occupations that were developed during the Industrial Revolution and trained so many people how to be authoritarian leaders are no longer accessible. Modernizing their operations, manufacturers started using machines instead of humans, which was more cost-effective and efficient. Technically competent individuals were more in demand as machines disappeared and robots took over the production floors.

Everything has a cause and effect connection; nothing occurs in a vacuum. A servant leader is aware of this and acts strategically. A servant leader is able to foresee this and take action to lessen the harm to their people. Losing a job results in a loss of income, and losing money results in losing security. Humans are capable of both reflection and planning, thus losing security can be very harmful to both the individual and the group as a whole. The harm to the community may be catastrophic when more and more individuals start to feel uneasy in their roles (inside the organization and the larger community). The loss of revenue to the region would have been disastrous had Shell UK decided to shut down its oil storage and pumping facilities in the UK. The servant leader ought to have expected this. The community should have been consulted, the servant leader should have been aware of their challenges, and the choice should have taken into account the community's future effects (foresight).

In the twenty-first century and beyond, the servant leader's position will grow, but it will also be enlarged. Some of these shifts have already been seen by people in professions that nearly demand a servant leader approach. Think about a teacher's job. Reading, writing, science, and math were taught by teachers when the area of education was consolidated in one place (a school with educators rather than learning and being taught by parents). Let it be known that teachers are generally born servant leaders whose first motivation is to improve the lives of children and their communities, not their own. The function of the teacher changed along with the evolution of the educational system. A student's academic development is no longer just the responsibility of the teacher. The need for both parents to work outside the house has increased as a result of parents' increased busyness in reaction to economic problems, leaving little support for a kid at home. Teachers must now operate "in loco parentis" (in the place of a parent) by providing their children with counseling and acting as a form of bank, all the while concentrating on teaching the youngster the survival skills. If a youngster is upset, they cannot learn. Since they are aware of this, teachers now have to assist the entire kid.

The same is true for business. The servant leader approach emphasizes the leader's efforts on the follower as a whole, rather than only on the abilities and problems linked to their position in the business. Managers who adhere to a servant leadership model find themselves in a similar position as teachers: encouraging their subordinates, supporting their willingness to advance professionally, and personally offering resources and mentoring when necessary. This is similar to how factory workers were made unemployed by the advent of machines and eventually robots.

The servant leader's job will evolve with the development of technology. The World Wide Web and the Internet's development have opened up markets that are far larger than those of conventional brick-and-mortar companies. In 2020, there were around 4.6 billion active Internet users worldwide (Clement, 2020). A requirement for labor results from this change in the market's size. Many corporations started to outsource the manufacture of their goods to other nations in an effort to reduce prices. Once again, this results in employment uncertainty, which is detrimental to the community as a whole.

A change in demands was also brought about by the growing dependence on technology and the Internet; instead of a significant need for human capital, a tremendous need for intellectual capital was established. A need for highly qualified individuals is knowledge capital. This makes it necessary for the servant leader to understand and empathize with their followers' needs. The servant leader, who serves as a mentor and motivator, recognizes the value of mentoring and has the tools necessary to gently encourage their followers to improve themselves.

The need for servant leaders rises along with population change and expansion. Two of the ten pillars of the servant leadership concept are listening and empathy. The organization won't last very long without a servant leader who has a solid grasp of the regional, cultural, and political views. The future servant leader must be exceptionally skilled at active listening, developing cognitive empathy, and comprehending the healing process. People are naturally sociable, and as a result, their social interactions and the values and customs of their communities change. The servant leader excels as a facilitator in this situation. The servant leader supports and works to better the people and places they live and work in by actively listening and by fostering an environment that values empathy and healing.

CONCLUSION

Animals have divided themselves into two groups over the course of time: leaders and followers. This resulted in the formation of a hierarchy. The leader group was made up of the creatures that were the strongest and wisest. While young, spirited animals regularly confront these animal leaders, the leader, being bigger and more strong, would be able to repel them. The cycle eventually repeats itself when old age and disease give way to the younger generations.

Animals are what we are, and strangely, the history of leadership in humans is both extremely similar and more nuanced. As far as science has revealed thus far, humans have sensations and emotions that other creatures just do not possess. In the animal world, a leader's only concern is guaranteeing the group's survival by locating food and shelter. Food, housing, and survival are concerns for people as well, but they also have complicated interpersonal interactions and job duties. Humans vary from other animals in that they may play a variety of roles, including those of parent, child, sibling, friend, manager, leader, and follower, and they have the ability to look back and forward in time.

The capacity for reflection on the past and foresight into the future while keeping in mind the lessons learned from the past. The essence of the human experience is this difficult process and how successfully one completes it. The servant leader's core competencies include the capacity to adapt these experiences to new contexts, the capacity to empathize and listen in order to understand others, the motivation to help others heal and feel whole, and the desire to improve individuals and communities.

Servant leaders recognize the value of being silent. A servant leader who keeps to themselves knows that in order to lead, one must first listen. A leader may better meet the requirements of their people by hearing and listening to them. A leader's ability to comprehend people and vice versa starts with listening. A servant must listen to the experiences and tales of their flock with an open heart and mind. Their ability to lead will increase if they demonstrate care, compassion, and active participation in a dialogue while learning from the viewpoints, experiences, and ideas of others. While a servant leader is always seeking to develop their abilities, more crucially, a servant leader cultivates connections with their followers. By listening, celebrating wins, and grieving losses, a servant leader fosters a feeling of community and a support system akin to a family. Allowing people to speak and have their voices heard is how a servant leader leads.

A leader must first comprehend their followers and develop empathy for other people once they have listened to and heard different viewpoints. Understanding other people's viewpoints and experiences is being sympathetic. Three types of empathy are discussed by various researchers: cognitive, emotional, and compassionate empathy. The capacity for cognitive empathy, also known as perspective-taking, is the capacity to comprehend another person's point of view; this is especially helpful in negotiations since it restricts the capacity for compassion. The most fundamental kind of empathy is emotional empathy. Pure emotion is necessary for emotional empathy, which enables a leader to "feel" the feelings of others. Negative emotional empathy may be seen as being too sympathetic or condescending, particularly when dealing with individuals from different racial, cultural, and socioeconomic backgrounds than the leader. This is true even if empathizing on an emotional level is advantageous in many respects.

Last but not least, compassionate empathy is the capacity to comprehend another person's feelings, "feel" their suffering, and then be inspired to act and provide assistance. Compassionate empathy is often the best kind of empathy to use while discussing servant leadership. While this can make it easier for leaders and followers to connect, it may also be seen as a nice medium between being under and too emotional.

Healing is another tenet of the servant leadership paradigm. Because it is in people's nature to dwell on happy and sad memories, feelings are just as real as the actual occurrence. Regardless of the cause of the suffering, the servant leader recognizes they must endeavor to create a culture of peace and healing. They have a philosophy of service first. A leader must foster a setting that promotes healing in order to do this. The servant leader essentially creates a team that feels more like a family. A leader should understand the requirements of their followers within the context of the mission's or team's objectives, as well as the knowledge that other things outside the team might have an effect on an individual. A leader must act on their knowledge and comprehension of the needs of their followers rather than acting for themselves in order to achieve this. A leader who is leading and guiding (healing) must put the needs of their followers first, handle the situation with empathy, and put in additional time and effort to help resolve the problem without thinking about their own self-interest.

The idea of awareness is also promoted by the servant-leadership paradigm. This first appears like a really straightforward concept. Being aware is a challenging and ever-evolving process for the servant leader since it affects both the team's overall and individual emotional health in addition to the success of their task. This implies that a leader has to spend time getting to know their followers as people, not merely as gears in a machine. A leader must first be aware of their own needs and trauma if the goal of awareness is to fulfill the needs of others. This is known as self-awareness (or internal awareness). In order to distinguish between what we need and what we want —as well as what we believe to be true about ourselves but may not really be—we must take a close, introspective look at ourselves.

Once a servant leader develops self-awareness, they must also develop exterior awareness—awareness of others around them. The servant leader must be conscious of how others see them as part of this. Because it enables a leader to comprehend every facet of their company and followers, external awareness is essential. Knowing their followers' emotional health and skill levels makes sense if a servant leader's primary motivation is to serve.

A leader must also be politically astute in order to follow the servant leader concept. Being politically aware entails being aware of group dynamics and how they develop and evolve. This implies that a servant leader must likewise be conscious of the problems and demands of the larger community. Knowing when to relinquish leadership of an organization and hand over responsibility for different areas of it to the most competent subordinates is another component of awareness. This enables the leader to spend the time necessary to get to know their followers personally and their community as a whole, in order to become aware of both groups' problems and needs.

Persuasion is a further tenet of the servant leadership paradigm. The ability to persuade is crucial if the ultimate objective of servant leadership is to create "better" individuals and stronger communities. Here, a servant leader utilizes persuasion to win over people and motivate them to take better care of themselves and their community. This is a challenging endeavor; a leader must persuade their supporters to believe in and comprehend the eventual result. Because of this, many servant leaders will have their organizations adopt a mission statement. A straightforward strategy to get everyone in the organization on the same page for a shared goal is to create a mission or vision statement. A mission/vision statement is a succinct declaration of an organization's purpose and the manner in which its members will interact with one another.

The servant leader believes that conceptualization provides an explanation for why. Leaders design and build companies, organizations, and volunteer organizations with a structure and objective in mind. This notion serves as the organization's main principle. A backwards (persuasive) mapping is a technique that many servant leaders adopt, stealing it from the realm of education. With the use of this tool, leaders must start the planning process by determining the purpose behind the formation of the organization, group, or company. The leader may next go on to organizing an organization's how after the why has been clarified. The method of backward planning is as simple as determining what actions must be taken to achieve and go beyond the ultimate result. The servant leader may conceptualize on their own. However, figuring out the necessary actions requires collaboration from all parties involved in the decision-making process.

The capacity to see into the future and foresee how their organization and actions will influence not just their followers but the community at large is what the servant-leader means by having foresight. Servant leaders must constantly reflect on the past and use the lessons they have learned to shape the future. To do this, a leader has to be able to draw lessons from prior failures and experiences, apply those lessons to their own and others' errors, and make the required modifications to the current job. Finally, they should consider the consequences—both positive and negative—and make the required changes to the idea, the plan, or both.

A servant leader's primary responsibility is to, well, serve others. At its core, servant leadership is about taking care of others. Stewardship, in the eyes of the servant leader, is all about fostering happiness for each individual inside a team or organization, as well as for the group as a whole and the community at large.

As crucial as the purpose itself is to the servant leader is taking care of their followers' needs and inspiring them to seek more for themselves—to take responsibility for their own personal and professional growth. The project objective and the measures required to attain it are the leader's top priorities in an authoritarian leadership approach.

The servant leader strives to strike a balance between fostering the growth of their followers on a personal, professional, and professional level while also ensuring that the current purpose is carried out successfully and positively impacts the community. To do this, a leader must inspire their people to pursue both professional and personal improvement while maintaining the organization's direction and progress. The servant leader must also make sure that their company has a good impact on the communities in which they operate.

Last but not least, the servant leader model aims to strike a favorable balance between showing a commitment to their followers and the larger community. According to this paradigm, a leader is dedicated to the development of their followers, and this dedication is subsequently returned. The followers of a servant leader who thinks that their followers' development comes first and foremost must care about the advancement of their leader and their company. A servant leader thinks that communities and followers both benefit from local growth. A leader must be sensitive to the requirements of the community as a whole in order for this to happen, in addition to the needs of their followers. Because of this, it's crucial for a servant leader to build strong relationships with their communities and followers.

Whether it be transactional or transformative, there are benefits and drawbacks to each of the many leadership approaches. Some approaches work better for immediate objectives. Other approaches to getting outcomes to take longer to develop. Being a servant leader is challenging. It requires dedication to time, a commitment to interacting with others, and the capacity to assign responsibility for a project to others. The servant leadership approach ultimately offers the finest framework for the sustained development of individuals, groups, and communities.

If you enjoyed this book and found some benefit in reading this, I'd like to hear from you and hope that you could take some time to post a review on Amazon. Your feedback and support will help this author to greatly improve his writing craft for future projects and make this book even better.

I want you, the reader, to know that your review is very important and so, if you'd like to leave a review, all you have to do is to scan the QR code and away you go.

I wish you all the best in your future success!

REFERENCES

- Al-Malki, M., & Juan, W. (2018). Impact of Laissez-Faire Leadership on Role Ambiguity and Role Conflict: Implications for Job Performance. INTERNATIONAL JOURNAL OF INNOVATION AND ECONOMIC DEVELOPMENT, 4(1), 29–43
- Anderson, G. (2014, May 7). The Servant Leader as a Healing Influence. The 16%; The 16%.
- Announcing the Dove Real Beauty Pledge. (2017, June 3). Unilever Global Company Website.
- Archer, R. L., & et al. (1981). The role of dispositional empathy and social evaluation in the empathic mediation of helping. Journal of Personality and Social Psychology, 40(4), 786–796.
- Babakus, E., Yavas, U., & Ashill, N. (2011). Service Worker Burnout and Turnover Intentions: Roles of Person-Job Fit, Servant Leadership, and Customer Orientation. Services Marketing Quarterly, 32(1), 17–31.

- Bacharach, S. (2005, May). Politically Proactive. Fast Company; Fast Company.
- Bacon, F. (n.d.). Essays, Civil and Moral: Vols. III, Part 1. The Harvard Classics.
- Barling, J., & Frone, M. R. (2016). If Only my Leader Would just DoSomething! Passive Leadership Undermines Employee Well-being Through Role Stressors and Psychological Resource Depletion. Stress and H
- Bass, B. M. (1985). Leadership and performance beyond expectations. Free Press ; London.
- Bass, R. R., & Bass, B. M. (2008). The Bass handbook of leadership : theory, research, and managerial applications. Free Press.
- bdl15. (2018, November 4). Servant leadership and an example of a VMV statement for an organization that employs servant leadership. Psu.Edu.
- Black, G. L. (2010). Correlational Analysis of Servant Leadership and School Climate. Journal of Catholic Education, 13(4), 437–466.
- Block, P. (1993). The empowered manager : positive political skills at work. John Wiley & Sons, Inc.
- BusinessDay. (2016, November 25). Warren buffett's servant leadership. Businessday NG.
- Cherry, K. (2020, August 3). What Are Prominent Leadership Styles and Frameworks You Should Know? (A. Morin, Ed.). Verywell Mind.
- Churchill, A., Barney, B., Hazel, A., Kelsall, D., Mouch, S., & Verdun, D. (2015). What is Stewardship, and should all great leaders practice it? « The New York Times in Education. Nytimesineducation.com.

- Ciulla, J. B., & James Macgregor Burns. (2014). Ethics, the heart of leadership. Praeger, An Imprint Of Abc-Clio, Llc.
- Clement, J. (2020). Internet users in the world 2020 | Statista. Statista; Statista.
- Commitment Staff. (2020, September 4). The power of servant leadership. Commitment.
- Conor Shine. (2019, January 3). Southwest Airlines' legendary co-founder Herb Kelleher dies at 87. Dallas News; The Dallas Morning News. ~:text=Kelleher%20-was%20also%20a%20formidable,friend%20and%20-client%20Rollin%20King.
- Cooper, K. (2018, July 3). Who Is The Servant Leader Really Serving? Forbes.
- Correlli, J. (2019, October 31). The 10 Principles of Servant Leadership | TeamGantt. Www.Teamgantt.com.
- Crick, B. (1993). In Defense of Politics (4th ed.). Chicago University Press.
- Crick, B. (2004). Politics as a for on rule: Politics, citizenship and democracy in Leftwich A (ed) What is politics. Cambridge: Polity Press.
- Dove Self-Esteem Project. (2020, April 8). Dove US.
- Edelman, B. G., Luca, M., & Svirsky, D. (2015). Racial Discrimination in the Sharing Economy: Evidence from a Field Experiment. SSRN Electronic Journal.
- Empathy Definition | What Is Empathy. (2009). Greater Good.
- Eurich, T. (2018, April 23). What Self-Awareness Really Is (and How to Cultivate It). Harvard Business Review.
- Fata, E. (2019, November 24). 5 Examples of Autocratic Leadership | Starting Business. Startingbusiness.com.

- Ferch, S. R. (2012). Forgiveness and power in the age of atrocity : servant leadership as a way of life. Lexington Books.
- Fisher, A. (2018, July 10). "Google Was Not a Normal Place": Brin, Page, and Mayer on the Accidental Birth of the Company that Changed Everything. Vanity Fair; Vanity Fair.
- Fitzpatrick, A. (2014, September 4). Google Used to Be the Company That Did "Nothing But Search." Time; Time.
- Fuller, T. (2000). Leading and leadership. University Of Notre Dame Press.
- Gandolfi, F. (2107, January). (PDF) Servant Leadership: An Ancient Style with 21 st Century Relevance. ResearchGate.
- Gibbons, M. (2019, February 26). 10 characteristics of servant leadership with quotes and questions. SkillPacks.
- Goleman, D. (2010). Emotional intelligence : why it can matter more than IQ. Bloomsbury.
- Green, S. (2015, October). Twitter.
- Greenleaf Center for Servant Leadership. (2016). What is Servant Leadership? - Greenleaf Center for Servant Leadership. Greenleaf Center for Servant Leadership.
- Greenleaf, R. (n.d.). Servant Leadershirp: A Journey ino the Natural Legitimate Po.
- Greenleaf, R. K., & Spears, L. C. (2002). Servant leadership : a journey into the nature of legitimate power and greatness. Paulist Press.
- Gregory Selden, et. al.m v AirBnb Inc, (US District of Court for the District of Columbia November 1, 2016).

- Griswold, A. (2016, June 23). The dirty secret of Airbnb is that it's really, really white. Quartz; Quartz.
- Guillaume, Dr. O. (2019). Leadership Strategicue; Transformer l'echec de votre enterprided en succes. Hartford Publishing.
- Hartley, J., & Branicki, L. (2006, October). Download Limit Exceeded. Citeseerx.Ist.Psu.Edu; Charter Management Institute.
- How Herb Kelleher Made the World a Whole Lot Smaller. (2019, January 5). Texas Monthly.
- Isaacson, W. (2011). Steve Jobs. Simon & Schuster.
- Kenton, W. (2019). Servant leadership. Investopedia.
- Kouzes, J. M., & Posner, B. Z. (1987). The Leadership challenge. Jossey-Bass.
- Labich, K., & Hadjian, A. (2020). IS HERB KELLEHER AMERICA'S BEST CEO? Behind his clowning is a people-wise manager who wins where others can't. - May 2, 1994. Fortune.com.
- Leander Kahney. (2019, April 16). How Steve Jobs finally persuaded a 37-year-old Tim Cook to join a near-bankrupt Apple in 1998. CNBC; CNBC.
- Lewin, K. (1939). Patterns of Aggressive Behavior in Experimentally Created "Social Climates." Journal of Social Psychology, 10(2), 271–299.
- Liden, R. C., Wayne, S. J., Zhao, H., & Henderson, D. (2008). Servant leadership: Development of a multidimensional measure and multi-level assessment. The Leadership Quarterly, 19(2), 161–177.
- Luca, M., & Bazerman, M. (2020, June 19). What data experiments tell us about racial discrimination on Airbnb. Fast Company.

- Mair, V. H. (1990). Tao Te Ching : The Classic Book of Integrity and The Way. Random House Publishing.
- Mar, R. A., Oatley, K., Hirsh, J., dela Paz, J., & Peterson, J. (2005). Bookworms versus nerds: Exposure to fiction versus non-fiction, divergent associations with social ability, ,and the simulation of fictional social worlds [Thesis]. In Google Docs.
- Mcdaniel, R. (2010, June 10). Understanding by Design. Vanderbilt University; Vanderbilt University.
- McDermott, T. (2004, June 6). Ronald Reagan Remembered. Cbsnews.com.
- Miller, K. (2018, September 5). Coaching Leadership Style Advantages, Disadvantages and Characteristics. FutureofWorking.com.
- Money-zine.com. (2020). Pacesetting Leadership. Money-Zine.com.
- Peters, T. J., & Waterman, R. H. (2015). In search of excellence : lessons from America's best-run companies. London Profile Books.
- Rai, R., & Prakash, A. (2012). A relational perspective to knowledge creation: Role of servant leadership. Journal of Leadership Studies, 6(2), 61–85.
- Ravinder, J., Sharma, C. S., & Kawatra, M. (2017). Healing a Broken Spirit: Role of Servant Leadership. Vikalpa: The Journal for Decision Makers, 42(2), 80–94.
- Rennaker, M. (2008). Listening and persuasion: Examining the communicative patterns of servant leadership [PhD Thesis].
- Riaz, A. (2019, February 20). Pacesetting Leadership. Inspired Trait; Inspired Trait.

- Rose Ngozi Amanchukwu, Gloria Jones Stanley, & Nwachukwu Prince Ololube. (2015). A Review of Leadership Theories, Principles and Styles and Their Relevance to Educational Management. Management, 5(1), 6–14.
- Schmidt, M. (2020, August 28). How Reading Fiction Increases Empathy and Encourages Understanding. Discover Magazine; Discover Magazine.
- Schoefolt, P. (2020). Wolves on Green Grass. In www.pexels.com.
- Schultz, H. (2018). Starbucks. Starbucks.com.
- Schwantes, M. (2020a, February 6). Warren Buffett Says Only 1 Trait Actually Points to a Great Leader. Inc.com; Inc.
- Schwantes, M. (2020b, February 6). Warren Buffett Says Only 1 Trait Actually Points to a Great Leader. Inc.com; Inc.
- Servant Leadership Examples & Characteristics. (2020, June 5). People Managing People.
- Servant Leadership in Action: Two Great Examples | Infosurv. (2017, July 28). Infosurv.
- Serve to Lead. (2013). Servant Leadership Quotations | Serve to Lead Group. Serve to Lead | James Strock.
- Sharma, S. (2013). What is Pacesetting Leadership? 4 Real-World Examples. Taskworld.
- Shoff, D. (n.d.). Servant Leader Principle #4 – Awareness – Leader As Servant. Leader as Servant. Retrieved December 10, 2020, from
- Shontell, A. (2011, January 19). - Business Insider. Business Insider; Business Insider.

- Spears, L. (1995). Reflections on Leadershp. John Wiley & Sons.
- Spears, L. (2019). Ten Characteristics of a Servant-Leader.
- Spears, L. (n.d.). Character and Servant Leadership: Ten Characteristics of Effective, Caring Leaders.
- Stempel, J. (2020, July 8). Warren Buffett donates $2.9 billion to Gates Foundation, family charities. U.S.
- Tarallo, M. (2018, May 17). The Art of Servant Leadership. SHRM; SHRM.
- The 'Dove Real Beauty Pledge. (2017a, March 2). The 'Dove Real Beauty Pledge.' Dove US.
- The 'Dove Real Beauty Pledge. (2017b, March 2). The 'Dove Real Beauty Pledge.' Dove US.
- Tobin, T. (2020). This Trendy Leadership Style Makes Employees Feel Valued — But It Also Poses a Risk to Managers. Fairygodboss.com.
- Types of Leadership Styles | Maryville Online. (2020). Maryville Online.
- United for Giving. (2016). Unitedhealthgroup.com.
- Valeri, D. (2007). THE ORIGINS OF SERVANT LEADERSHIP.
- Viva Differences. (2020, January 29). Active Listening Vs Passive Listening: 8 Major Differences With Examples. Viva Differences.
- What is Stewardship, and should all great leaders practice it? « The New York Times in Education. (2015). Nytimesineducation.com.
- Wheeler, D. W. (2011). Servant leadership for higher education : principles and practices. Jossey-Bass.

- Wiggins, G. (2012). UNDERSTANDING BY DESIGN ® FRAMEWORK.
- Wolf Pack Hierarchy - Facts about the Wolf Social Structure. (2014). Wolffacts.org.

Made in United States
Orlando, FL
06 December 2022

25627816R00065